TELEVISION AND THE CHRISTIAN HOME

by Marvin Moore

PACIFIC PRESS PUBLISHING
ASSOCIATION
Mountain View, California
Omaha, Nebraska   Oshawa, Ontario

Copyright © 1979 by
Pacific Press Publishing Association
Litho in United States of America
All Rights Reserved

Library of Congress Catalog Card No. 78-71157

Preface

Social scientists have carried out hundreds of studies investigating the impact of television on our society. Crime is an epidemic in America, and much of the research on television has focused on the influence of televised violence on children and young people. Students make lower scores on aptitude tests, particularly verbal scores. Is television in any way to blame for that? What about the psychological effects of TV? What about sex? Some people ask if there's anything good at all about television.

For the Christian, one question overrides all others: What is the impact of television on my character and on my relationship to Christ? What place, if any, should television have in my home? Are there Biblical guidelines that I can follow in controlling the set in my living room?

This book is not an investigation of all the research on all the issues about television. It is rather a summary of the major issues as they relate to the Christian way of life. Television is a threat to the Christian's relationship with God, just as it is a threat to education and to law and order. But it doesn't have to be. Used with discretion, it can enhance the Christian life. I hope what I have said will help many Christians to make a more constructive use of the television set in their homes.

Marvin Moore
February 10, 1978

Table of Contents

1 What Is TV? 9
2 The Ominous Equation 14
3 The Atmosphere of the Home 22
4 Television and Children 26
5 Television, Violence, and Crime 30
6 The Industry's View of Violence 47
7 Christianity and Violence 55
8 Television and Sex 60
9 The Positive Effects of Television 67
10 Television and the School 73
11 Television and You 80
   You Can Help Change TV 92

1

What Is TV?

Suppose Buck Rogers's little green Martians really existed. And suppose that on a swing through the solar system they chanced to pass near enough to the earth to pick up one of our television programs. Let's suppose they became so fascinated with TV that they watched another program, and another, and another. What impression might they get of us earthlings?

Certainly they would discover what we look like: head, face, arms and legs, hands and feet, men, women and children, shirts and skirts. They would also know that our civilization is highly technological. They would see cars and planes, electric lights, tall buildings with elevators, and some sort of wire mesh sticking over the roof of every home in the land.

But what would they learn about our ideas? Our values? The things we are most interested in?

Perhaps they would think we like to laugh a lot or love a lot or both. If they happened by at five or ten p.m., they might decide we are interested in what is going on in the world. Depending on the program they watched, they would think coyotes were fascinated by roadrunners or that they scarcely pay them any attention at all. Would the Martians think we are basically a law-abiding civilization? Or would they conclude that it takes an immense police force to maintain order? And would they consider the cops or the robbers to be the most inhumane in their treatment of other human beings? What would they conclude was most important to us: kindness and courtesy, or power and possession?

A Nigerian who tuned in to an American TV drama said, "I did not realize that Americans valued human life so little."

At the beginning of 1976 nearly 70 million American homes—97 percent—had at least one working television set. The average home operated a TV six and a half hours each day. Nobody can accuse the TV of failure to put in a full week's work! The average American child watches television three to four hours a day, and one fourth spend more than five hours a day, seven days a week, in front of the set.[1] By the time he starts to school, the average American child has spent more time in front of the TV than a college student spends in the classroom. By the time he graduates from high school, he will have spent more time watching TV than watching his own teacher. Among major activities only sleep and work consume more of the average person's time than television.

The total purchase price of America's combined television sets is more than $15 billion, with an equal amount invested in repairs. The cost of operating these sets (electricity) runs into millions of dollars each year. American industry spends $5 billion annually for commercial advertisements and another $13 billion for program development.[2] America is not getting its television entertainment free!

Where did this fantastic invention come from?

The basic scanning principle on which TV is based was first proposed about 1880 by W. E. Sawyer in the United States and Maurice Leblanc in France. A German scientist, Paul Nipkow, patented the first proposal for a complete television system in 1884. Boris Rosing, a Russian scientist, was one of the first to create an image on the screen. In 1907 he succeeded in reproducing crude geometric figures. In 1908 the basic principles on which modern television is based were outlined by Campbell-Swinton, a Scottish electical engineer. An American scientist, Vladimir Zworvkin, developed an electronic tube in 1923 that later became important in the TV camera.

NBC began operating an experimental television station in New York City on July 30, 1930, and CBS followed about a year later. Regular broadcasting service began in Germany in 1935, though the image was very crude. Under the direction of Sir Isaac Shoenberg, Britain established the first high-quality broadcasting system in 1936—a system that retained its basic features until 1964. Regular commercial broadcasting began in the United States in New York City on April 30, 1939. Production of television sets ceased during World War II, but refinement of the overall system continued, so that rapid expansion was possible when broadcasting resumed in 1946. By 1949 Americans owned one million sets, and that number had jumped to ten million by 1951. There are well over 100 million television sets in the United States today, and the figure worldwide is close to 300 million.

Back in 1900 most people thought Henry Ford's car was a handy substitute for the horse and carriage. But the impact of the automobile on American life has gone far beyond replacing wagons. It has been largely responsible for our shift from an agrarian to an industrial economy, from a country society to a nation of city dwellers. Seventy-five years after Ford built the first car, America had all but completed the most massive public works project in history to accommodate his invention: the interstate freeway system. The Conestoga wagon crossed the continent in six months. The car covers the same distance in three to four days of steady freeway driving. America has been welded together by, among other things, the car.

Yet the impact of television has been greater. Little did Nipkow realize the impact his idea would have on America and the world when he patented the first idea for TV in 1884. The car moves the body about the neighborhood or across the nation. Television carries the mind around the world in an instant. The car affects where we go. Television affects what we think. Television controls when we eat and sleep and when (or whether) we study the Bible and go to church. Television has even forced the redesign of several large city water systems to accommodate the huge drain when everyone rushes to the bathroom during prime-time commercial breaks.[3] In 1975 *U.S. News and World Report* asked 1000 American men and women of distinction what institution they considered to be the most powerful in the nation. Television ranked third—after the White House and the Supreme Court. And a 1974 poll put television in first place. The radio, books, magazines, and newspapers exert a powerful influence on our culture, but TV is unquestionably the greatest single force reflecting and molding attitudes and behavior in our society. Yet thirty years ago most Americans had not even seen one! We speak of educational TV as though it were special. All TV is educational. The only question is, What does it teach?

What is TV doing to our society? What is its potential? And how should the Christian relate to these issues? That is what this book is all about.

2
The Ominous Equation

I am a house-husband. My wife goes off to work each morning, and I stay home. No, I am not liberated, and neither is she. I am a writer, and my office is at one end of the house. I get a unique insight, though, into some of the problems that *wives* go through, not the least of which is the *joy* of swallowing my own cooking when she doesn't come home to lunch. (When she does, which is most of the time, she fixes it).

I hate to cook for myself. I detest eating alone. I will keep pecking the keys on my typewriter till two or three in the afternoon just to avoid the trauma of pasting together my own cold, tasteless sandwich. But at three o'clock one afternoon I finally yielded to my stomach and stumbled to the refrigerator to see what I could scrounge that might be good. By definition, "good" was anything that tasted like fun, regardless of its nutritional qualifications. I was in no mood to spend a lot of time fixing. I had nearly finished eating when I finally stopped long enough to think about what I had culled from the refrigerator and the cupboard. The discovery left me numb: two cookies, two fig bars, Fritos, eight or ten small marshmallows, roasted peanuts, and a small bowl of yogurt.

I didn't die, and I wouldn't if I did a rerun. What troubled me was not the prospect of immediate death from my unhealthful diet, but the realization that I'd succumbed to something so foolish: impulse eating. My meal was inspired by my tastebuds and goaded on by my stomach's insistent demands. Save for the yogurt (it was plain, which helped relieve the guilt) and perhaps the peanuts, everything else was "junk food."

America's TV diet is disconcertingly similar to my hasty lunch that afternoon. We pore over the *TV Guide* scrounging for something good to watch, "good" meaning anything that will entertain the eyes and ears, not what might be nutritious for the mind and the spirit. The TV producers and the advertisers are well aware of the human propensity for entertainment. That's why the vast majority of TV shows today are just that: entertainment. Even the so-called educational programs for children ("Sesame Street," "Electric Company," etc.) rely on entertainment to get the kids' attention. The producers know there are certain things guaranteed to entertain: competition, violence, sex, humor, drama, and suspense.

Two plus two equals—and any school boy can come up with the answer—four. TV's ominous equation isn't much more complicated than that. Proctor and Gamble wants to sell soap. ABC wants to sell TV time. Add the two together and you get entertainment: whatever is the lowest common denominator fare the public will rush to their sets to watch. And Nielsen is the magic mathematician that tells whether the answer is right or wrong.

It works like this.

The advertiser needs to expose people's eyes and

ears to the sights and sounds of his product. Television delivers the message right into the living rooms of seventy-three million American homes. With three television networks in America, each is out to persuade the nation's top advertisers that it can produce the most viewers. A lot of people think the basic purpose of the networks is to broadcast programs. It is not. The networks are big business, just like General Motors or IBM. Their basic objective is to make a profit. General Motors makes its profit by selling cars. IBM sells computers. The networks sell people—people's eyes and ears to see and hear the advertiser's commercial.

The program? That's just the bait to get you and me to tune in the set. The TV industry and the advertisers want us hooked to their programs so we will watch their commercials. And what's the hook? Our likes. Our emotions. Whatever fascinates us the most. Whatever entertains us enough that we leave the set turned on.

Did you ever read in the newspaper that fifty-three million people watched the President's press conference? Or that CBS's "All in the Family" drew two million more viewers than ABC's "Sunday Night Movie" and three million more than NBC's "Bionic Woman?" And did you ever wonder how anyone ever arrived at those figures?

The A. C. Nielsen Company of Chicago contracts with about 1200 families in different parts of the United States to attach a little black box to the family's television set. The box, hooked by direct line to a computer in Dunedin, Florida, monitors the set twenty-four hours a day. The computer knows exactly when the set is turned on, what programs the family watches, and when they turn the set off. Switch channels, and

Nielsen's computer records it for posterity. Twice each day the computer prepares a composite of all programs watched by all its families, and like any polling institution, projects the figures nationwide. The TV industry pays a heavy price for the information Nielsen provides, because it is their only way of finding out the effectiveness of their programs.

Some programs are more popular than others, and more people tune in at certain times of the day. Prime time, when more people watch TV than at any other, includes from seven to nine p.m., with weekends drawing the largest prime-time audience. Nielsen rates programs according to percentage points. An 18.0 rating means 18 percent of the nation's seventy-three million television homes watched a particular program. An 18.0 rating is the bottom line figure for a prime-time program to survive. A 20.0 rating nets the company $150,000 for a one-minute spot, compared to half that figure for a 15.0 rating. The economics of these figures are obvious! During an entire season a popular program may be worth $3 million more than a program with a low rating.

Children will choose their potatoes in chips rather than mashed any day, unless Mom and Dad are there to force the issue. Most adults have learned to eat what is good for them whether they like it or not, at least part of the time. But it is seldom that way with TV. The average person pays almost no attention to what is best for his mind when he turns on his set. Whatever is most amusing or most exciting, that is what he watches. The TV industry's basic objective is to catch the viewer's fancy, because that is what brings the most dollars from the sponsors. And that is the ominous equation, ominous because of the implications for America's moral and spiritual future. If TV is the most powerful cultural force in our nation today, and if TV's moral impact is ruled by our fancy rather than by our intelligent choice of worthwhile programming, what can we expect the next generation to be like, and the next after that? A diet of junk food flatters the taste buds, but it ruins the body. A diet of junk programming flatters the eyes and ears, but it ruins the soul.

Obviously, the easiest place to control program content is at the network level. Theoretically. But the networks are not interested in any change that will drop ratings. Said one program producer, "All the network people do is line up the programs on their long table and juggle them against the competition (competing network programs), asking, 'What will work best against that?' "

For years, ABC was the tail in the television industry. Then in 1977 it zoomed into first place, leaving CBS and NBC coughing in its dust. As of this writing ABC claims the four top-rated shows on the market and seven of the top ten. CBS has two of the top ten, and NBC one. At CBS, the leader for 20 years, higher-echelon heads toppled like bowling pins. Yet the whole industry is in trouble. During the last half of 1977 total TV viewing on all stations and networks dropped 3.4 percent each month. *Time* magazine said, "No one knows why [the sudden drop], but advertisers are watching keenly. If it continues, more shakeups will be in store."[2] Reason? To save those advertising dollars. If the trend has reversed by the time this book is in print, the point has not: keep up those ratings.

Any righteous moralizing about program content gets short shrift in a climate like that. The industry's only caution is to avoid overshock. Said Douglas Cater in his *TV Violence and the Child,* "Although they [industry programmers] claimed to keep up with social science research, they refused to acknowledge that it has any practical value for their judgments. . . . Censors are not basically motivated by any great social conscience."[3]

David L. Bazelon, Chief Judge of the U.S. Court of Appeals for the District of Columbia Circuit, hears all appeals from the licensing decisions of the Federal Communications Commission. In an address before the Federal Communications Bar Association, Bazelon said, "I think they [industry representatives] know the times they have prostituted the tremendous potential of television as a human communication tool. They know what should be done about it. The programming executives and their advertiser clients must stop their single-minded purpose to achieve higher ratings, more advertising and greater profits, and stop to consider what greater purposes television should serve. And they must do it soon if we are to preserve the First Amendment values for telecommunications."[4]

What Bazelon means is that unless the industry censors itself, the government may have to. Freedom from censorship lies at the foundation of the First Amendment—freedom of the press. Yet sensitive as journalists, editors, and broadcasters are about censorship, some are already beginning to talk about it as imperative to preserve our American way of life. The liberal author, Walter Lippmann, said, "A continual exposure of a generation to the commercial exploitation of the enjoyment of violence and cruelty is one way to corrode the foundations of a civilized society. For my own part, believing as I do in freedom of speech and thought, I see no objection in principle to censorship of the mass entertainment of the young. Until some more refined way is worked out of controlling this evil thing, the risks of our liberties are, I believe, decidedly less than the risks of unmanageable violence."[5]

There are two sides to every story, and the TV industry takes a firm stand in defense of its programming policies. One of the most controversial programs in recent times is ABC's "Soap," a sex-saturated spoof of day-time soap operas. The Southern Baptist Convention, Methodists, the United Church of Christ—even the liberal National Council of Churches—joined in opposing "Soap" prior to its introduction in the 1977-78 season. But, "I believe that 'Soap' will present very positive models and will lead," said ABC's program director, Fred Silverman. "I say that because I think that the underpinning of the show is the sanctity of the family unit—believe it or not. There is a scene between a mother and her daughter that will make you cry. Now my feeling is that if you can get involved enough in a program that when two of the characters start communicating with each other to the point where you're moved—then that's a good program."[6]

Silverman is probably sincere. Television industry leaders have not deliberately set out to ruin America's morals. Wendy Ehrlich summed up the industry's dilemma well in the book, *Children's Television: The Economics of Exploitation*. She said, "As a 'public trustee,' the broadcaster is constantly placed in the position of weighing the conflicting objectives of economic profit and public service. He must attempt to make the system serve two generally conflicting masters."[7] Who of us would do better were we in Silverman's shoes or anyone else's in television's top echelons?

An ominous equation exists in our television industry that we need to do something about. But merely castigating the industry is not the answer. There is no one answer for any one person. Each American needs to think in terms of alternative answers for himself, out of which may grow *the* answer for us all.

3

The Atmosphere of the Home

In a tour of a hospital a couple of friends stopped at the nursery and spent a few minutes watching a red-faced, newborn baby in a crib by the window. They joked about "his worries," and how nice it would be if they had his instead of theirs.

What is the first sight of light to a baby's eyes? Before birth it heard its mother's heartbeat and a few muffled sounds from the outside world. It felt, perhaps, the touch of its own hands here and there on its skin. It tasted the salty water inside the womb. And that's about all a baby's world amounts to when it's born. That is an infant's mind.

A baby's mind is empty, to be filled. The filling goes on till death, but each passing year the filling mixes with more and more of what went before, and makes less and less of its original impression on the mind. What comes first counts most. God made babies with brand new minds, and He made homes for them to grow in. The first filling of the mind takes place in the home, those first sights and sounds that leave their own impressions and nothing more. God tells us what those sights and sounds ought to be: "These commandments which I give you this day are to be kept in your heart;

you shall repeat them to your sons, and speak of them indoors and out of doors, when you lie down and when you rise. Bind them as a sign on the hand and wear them as a phylactery on the forehead; write them up on the doorposts of your houses and upon your gates" (Deuteronomy 6:6-9, *The New English Bible*).

Notice the broad similarity with television: constant exposure, day after day, year after year.

Television preempts the program God planned for children's minds when He placed them in homes. The TV set is on six to seven hours a day in the average American home. The time element is like God's plan. God did not expect the Israelites to read the Bible and pray six or seven hours a day, but He did expect parents to keep the principles of right living prominent in their children's daily work and play. The parents' chief concern was to be the content of the lessons impressed on their children's developing minds, not just at Bible-reading time but *all* the time.

The publishers of *The New English Bible* won't mind a slight revision of their text, "This television set that I give you this day is to be kept in your living room; you shall turn it on for your sons, and let them watch it indoors and out of doors, when they lie down and when they rise." That is exactly how it is in some homes. The TV goes on in the morning when the kids get up, and it is left on the rest of the day. Television is a constant influence in the home.

There is also significant similarity in content between television and the Bible. From cover to cover the Bible is filled with lessons about life and the right and wrong way to live. From six a.m. to twelve midnight the TV is filled with its version of right and wrong. The

Bible is largely stories. So is TV. God knew the human fascination with stories, and He knew the moral impact of stories on the mind. God's instruction to the Israelites to keep his commandments before their children included repeating over and over the stories of the Bible.

Christianity is not merely a set of doctrines, or a list of rules and regulations, though there is an advantage in expressing it this way for certain purposes. Christianity is a way of life. It is a way of thinking that begins at birth and ends at death. It is the things that fill the mind. That's why God planned for spiritual and moral lessons to make up a large part of that filling, beginning very early in life. How can sights and sounds at age thirty be mixed with a strong Christian flavor if the Christian flavor was not introduced into the mind at ages one, six, and ten?

Television carries a message about morality and how to live, but there's a difference. God's plan for filling children's minds is primarily concerned with what is best for the child. Television's plan is primarily concerned with what is best for the advertiser, the network, and the station. God's plan teaches children and adults to control their impulses. Television hooks the fancies and the desires in order to sell something. There are very few lessons on TV about self-control. Yet that is the first lesson of life that every child needs to learn and that God's plan teaches.

The home that follows God's plan emphasizes His moral and spiritual values through the day. The windows are not made of stained glass and there's not a pulpit in every room. What matters is the things family members say to each other and their behavior through the day. And it is difficult if not impossible to have the TV blaring six to seven hours a day, occupying the minds of family members with crime or trivia, and expect to have God's atmosphere too. This is not to say that there are not worthwhile programs for the Christian to watch. But these must be selected for the contribution they will make to the Christian atmosphere. They don't come in a steady stream just by turning on the TV and letting it run the rest of the day. The person who wants the home God described in Deuteronomy 6:6-9 must take charge of his television. Turning off the TV is not a straight path to sanctification. But it helps.

How to make television contribute to the right atmosphere in the home is part of the challenge of being a Christian in the last half of the twentieth century.

4
Television and Children

Hundreds of studies have been conducted in the last few years investigating the impact of television on society. Most of these have dealt with the effect of TV on children. Much of what is discussed in the rest of this book is about the effects of TV on children in specific areas. However, certain general principles need to be covered first.

Do children understand stories? Children at different ages interpret the data of television differently. Children begin paying a significant amount of attention to television between their first and second birthdays. However, their understanding of what they see remains incomplete throughout the preschool years and into early elementary school. They may be fascinated with a program, yet fail to understand the plot. Tell a four-year-old a simple story, then ask him to repeat it. He will probably mix up the sequence of events, and repeat points that seemed important to him but were not basic to the story. First and second graders remember simple stories, but still cannot grasp the more complex plots in movies and TV dramas.

Do children understand moral implications? Young children are especially impressed by the results of an action, regardless of why it happened. A social scientist experimented with two groups of children: one group of very young children and another group of ten- and eleven-year-olds. He told each group two stories. The first story described a character who did something that caused little damage, but which was done for the wrong reason. In the second story the character's action was well intended, but it caused considerable damage. To the young children, the person causing the least damage was the best person. The ten- and eleven-year-olds judged the stories according to the characters' intentions.[1] The tendency of young children to approve of results regardless of motive has been found to apply fairly consistently to their viewing of television stories.

Television stories are much more complex than the stories in the experiment just mentioned. They involve many actions, and the results may be a mixture of good and bad. Evaluating a television story requires not only the ability to judge motive and consequences, but to weigh their relative importance. Older children can do this, but young ones cannot.

Modeling. Children imitate adults. This process is called "modeling." Children use television characters as models. One study exposed children to both TV and live models, some good and others bad. Researchers concluded that "the effect of televised example was generally as potent as that of live example," and "both of these types of observational experiences were more important influences on the child's rule breaking than live verbal statements presented by an adult."[2] Tested a month later, children in the group exposed to bad TV models were still more likely to break a rule than children in a control group who were not exposed to the bad model. Comments Robert Liebert of the department of psychology at the State University of New York, "This demonstration that a brief exposure can instill a remarkably stable tendency to transgress provides strong refutation of the argument that television examples exert only highly transitory influences on moral behavior."[3]

This is particularly significant in that if a child fails to catch the cues that would place an action in a proper moral context, it is possible that he might imitate according to the results of a model's behavior rather than according to its moral context.

Advertisers and television industry representatives tend to downplay effects of negative TV programming on children's behavior. However, these same advertisers spend billions of dollars each year on the assumption that their TV commercials *will* affect the behavior of both children and adults. One company's sales mushroomed from $300 million in 1952 to $1.8 billion in 1965 as a result of television advertising.[4] Obviously, television influenced somebody's behavior! Modeling is one of the important ways that behavior is influenced. Studies indicate that the amount of time spent in front of the TV is as important as the kind of program viewed.[5] The more a child watches a particular model, the more that model's behavior will be reinforced in his mind, and the more likely he will be to imitate it.

God knew the importance of modeling to a child's moral development. That is why He said to the Israelites, "You shall repeat them [My laws] to your sons, and speak of them indoors and out of doors, when you lie down and when you rise" (Deuteronomy 6:7, *The New English Bible*). God planned for children to grow up in a moral environment dominated by biblical principles of life, with biblically committed adults as models. Is that the moral environment TV brings into your home? What is TV teaching your children? More important, what are you *allowing* TV to teach your children?

5
Television, Violence, and Crime

Evelyn Wagler ran out of gas a couple of blocks from her home in Boston. It was a Tuesday evening in October 1973. The only service station in the area was closed; so she walked eleven blocks to another station down the street. A gallon can of gas in hand, she started back. She hurried past liquor stores, restaurants, and apartment buildings. Couples strolled in the evening, and drunks loitered in the shadows.

Shortly before she reached her car, six youths attacked her. They dragged her to a vacant lot behind an apartment house and told her to pour the gasoline over her body. She refused. They threatened, and she obeyed. One of the boys lit a match and threw it at her. Instantly, her body was aflame. She rolled on the ground, threw dirt on the flames, and managed to put out the fire, but the smoldering clothes now burned into her flesh. She walked calmly to the street, past several shops, to a liquor store. "Please call an ambulance," she said to the clerk, who stared at her in disbelief. The clerk called for an ambulance and the police, and brought a blanket. By then several customers had picked off most of the smoldering sweater still sticking to her blackened skin. Four hours later Evelyn Wagler died in the Boston City Hospital.

This is a horrible story. Equally as shocking is the cause of the senseless crime. News reports denied either robbery or sexual assault as the motive. But Boston's TV viewing citizens were quick to point out an obvious possibility: the motion picture *Fuzz*, telecast nationwide just 48 hours before, including over Boston's Channel 5. The film, supposedly comic, included a scene in which young Boston hoodlums set fire to derelict winos. Nobody got hurt on Sunday evening's performance, not even the actors who were "burned up" during the shooting of the film. But Tuesday evening Evelyn Wagler became a real human torch, and within six hours she was dead.

This incident dramatically illustrates a question of increasing concern in America: the effect of televised violence on our society, and particularly on our children and young people.

One of the most striking TV-to-crime relationships is that of *The Doomsday Flight* shown on NBC several years ago. The plot involves a bomb placed on a passenger airplane, with a threat from the bomber to blow up the plane unless he is paid a large ransom. A major airline received an identical bomb threat while the program was still on the air. Four similar threats were made within the next twenty-four hours, and eight more were received by the end of the week. Australia aired the film, and Qantas Airlines coughed up half a million dollars ransom in response to a bomb threat against 116 passengers on a plane bound for Hong Kong. In every case, the technique in real life was identical to that on the TV program.

The case for TV and violent crime has even been

taken to court. On June 4, 1977, fifteen-year-old Ronald Zamora and a friend burglarized the home of a neighbor in Miami, Florida. When the eighty-two-year-old woman confronted the boys, they shot her to death with a gun they had found in her own home. Four days later Zamora confessed to the murder. His attorney argued in court that the youth was innocent because of "subliminal television intoxication." Zamora's parents acknowledged that the boy was a confirmed TV addict who spent at least six hours a day in front of the set. His favorite programs were crime dramas such as "Kojak," "Baretta," and "Starsky and Hutch." The boy refused to eat unless the TV was turned on.

Crime has been a growing problem in America for years, particularly crime committed by young people. During the first half of the 1970s crime by ten- to seventeen-year-olds rose twice as fast as adult crime. During the mid-70s juveniles committed half of all serious crime, including murders, rapes, aggravated assaults and robbery. In San Francisco 56 percent of all felonies against people and 66 percent of all crimes against property were committed by juveniles, and in Chicago a full third of all murders during 1976 were committed by people 20 and under. In New York City 4449 children under the age of 16 were arrested for robbery during 1973, 181 for rape, and 94 for murder. "It is as though our society had bred a new genetic strain, the child murderer, who feels no remorse and is scarcely conscious of his acts,"[1] wrote one analyst. In a reenactment of the Evelyn Wagler murder, a six-year-old boy in Washington, D.C., siphoned gasoline from a car, poured it over a sleeping neighbor, lit a match, and stood by to watch the man go up in flames.

"It takes a diligent search through history to discover another society that has been as vulnerable to its youthful predators," says *Time* magazine's Edwin Warner in a cover story on youth crime in the July 11, 1977, issue.[2] And the motive is often mindless. Warner quotes a Manhattan youngster who told him that mugging "is like playing a game." The kids often have more money (from selling drugs, from other robberies, etc.) than the people they attack. Yet they go on attacking. "You know, they don't wanta be wearin' the same old sneakers every day," said one juvenile. "They wanta change, like, you know, they wanta pair of black sneakers."[3]

Nobody suggests that violence on television is the sole cause of the problem. Ghetto life in the cities, frustration over poverty and unemployment, alcohol and drugs, the breakdown of family life, lax punishment against juvenile offenders (or none at all) by the courts—these and other factors are unquestionably involved. However, most people recognize that televised violence plays a significant role in the rising crime rate, particularly among children and youth. Evelyn Wagler's torch murder in Boston seems so obviously to have stemmed from the *Fuzz* telecast two days earlier that it is hardly worth debating.

The amount of violent crime on television is staggering. The average American child will have watched 18,000 TV murders by the time he is eighteen years of age. And that is just murders. A CBS "Friday Night Movie" in January 1976 featured "three shootings resulting in injuries, four attempted shootings, two shoot-outs, nine threatened shootings, two armed break-ins, three other displays of guns, one shooting of a phone booth, one attempted strangling, four death threats, six armed assaults, four other assaults, five fights, one display of a corpse, one purse-snatching, and several displays of destruction of a building by a wrecking crew while police rookies chased drug dealers through the place."[4]

Hard proof that violence on TV spawns crime in the streets is hard to come by. However, by 1968 the national government officials had become sufficiently alarmed that President Johnson appointed the National Commission on the Causes and Prevention of Violence under the chairmanship of Dr. Milton Eisenhower. And in 1969, at the request of Senator John Pastore, the Department of Health, Education and Welfare established the Surgeon General's Scientific Committee on Television and Social Behavior.

The Eisenhower Commission reported: "A large body of research on observational learning by preschool children . . . confirms [that] children can and do learn aggressive behavior from what they see in a film or on a TV screen. . . . The vast majority of experimental studies . . . have found that observed violence stimulates aggressive behavior rather than the opposite. We do not suggest that television is a principal cause of violence in society. We do suggest that it is a contributing factor. . . . It is a matter of grave concern that at a time when the values and the influence of traditional institutions such as family, church, and school are in question, television is emphasizing violence, antisocial styles of life."[5]

Surgeon General Jesse Steinfeld, reporting on his committee's findings, stated, "While the committee report is carefully phrased and qualified in language acceptable to social scientists, it is clear to me that the causal relationship between televised violence and antisocial behavior is sufficient to warrant appropriate and immediate remedial action."[6] The senior research coordinator on the staff of the Surgeon General's Committee, Dr. George Comstock, said, "The most scientifically justifiable conclusion, given the available evidence, is that violent television entertainment increases the probability of subsequent aggressive behavior on the part of children and youth."[7]

Psychologists believe that televised violence produces the following four changes in viewers, and particularly in children:

1. It teaches the techniques of crime to many who otherwise would never have thought of those methods.
2. It increases aggressive behavior.
3. It increases the tolerance of aggressive behavior.
4. It distorts reality.

The Techniques of Crime. Several years ago, I edited the weekly newspaper in the small community where I live. My local police chief reported to me a raid he and the county sheriff made on a local gang of youthful criminals about twenty miles out in the country. He told me how the law enforcement officers learned of the gang's headquarters, how they approached it, and how they conducted their raid. And he described the weapons and other criminal evidence they found on the premises. One of the most interesting finds was a unique bomb set to explode and kill under special conditions. He described the bomb to me in some detail. And I, without considering the possible consequences, gave a piece-by-piece description of the device in my newspaper report. It was merely a part of the total story that I thought local people would find interesting.

Just how interesting, I soon found out. A few days later a young man accosted me and congratulated me on the article. "And that bomb those fellows made—that was really clever!" he exclaimed. "Why, I'd never thought of using . . . before and putting it with. . . ." (For obvious reasons, I prefer not to descibe the device here and repeat the mistake). He proceeded to explain, in quite scientific terms, exactly why the device was so effective. I was horrified! I had heard of bomb instruction manuals circulated by underground terrorist groups, but it had never occurred to me that I would contribute to them. Had the thought crossed my mind while writing the article, I would have cut that part immediately.

All I did was to describe the construction of an explosive device in a news report—with mere words. What techniques do sinister minds all over the country pick up from the daily flood of crime that pours out of 120 million television sets! Man's inventiveness is a gift bestowed on him by the Creator, and it is a talent of the entire human race, not just the criminals. TV writers, intent on coming up with a new twist, can be just as clever with their imaginations as the criminals. Often, unique methods that a writer himself describes only for the entertainment of the viewer suggest to the criminal a new way of carrying on his business that he would otherwise never have thought of. In my business of writing I depend heavily on the writing of others to spawn new creative ideas in my mind. What housewife hasn't visited the neighbor or a relative across town and discovered some "neat new way" to cook this or freeze that? Are we to suppose that the criminal is exempt from such adaptations from the inventiveness of others?

Of course not! Even children catch on. One eight-year-old rattled off to a social worker a long list of weapons that could be used to kill people. He concluded by saying, "I wouldn't have known about these things if I didn't watch TV."[8]

Increased Aggressive Behavior. Scientists don't have too much trouble analyzing a rock in the laboratory, a sample of spring water, or a scrap of newsprint. Science laboratories around the world routinely determine the physical and chemical makeup of all kinds of material. Modern medicine, space travel, and our worldwide communication systems are proof of the effectiveness of these experiments.

Social science research is much more difficult to conduct. Social science investigates ideas, attitudes, and relationships between people. Fire experts may determine exactly what caused a building to burn during an inner-city race riot: a Molotov cocktail, perhaps, or a bomb hurled through a window. But determining the human, emotional factors that caused residents to burn up their own community may be almost impossible. People, including the ones who rioted, are very quick to give reasons. But often the real reasons lie buried deep in human minds, in social forces that at first glance may not even be apparent. It is easy to say, "This is the cause of that." And often there is an element of truth to these intuitive conclusions. Few people will question the relationship between the *Fuzz* telecast in Boston and Evelyn Wagler's death, or between *The Doomsday Flight* telecast and the half million dollars that Qantas Airlines was forced to cough up as ransom. But these are isolated instances, committed by mentally unbalanced persons. The question that concerns the average parent around the country is whether televised violence will affect an otherwise normal child in an adverse manner. And are adults immune just because they are older? Are all affected by violence, or just a few?

Hundreds of research projects have been conducted involving thousands of human subjects, particularly children, to find the answers to these questions. And the answers are coming in. There is now no question that violence on television affects the behavior of everybody, and especially of children.

Before discussing the research we need to define one term: "aggressive behavior." "Aggressive behavior" as defined by the social scientist means any action that is either hostile or harmful to one's own self or to others. The likelihood of children with such behavior patterns turning to crime is assumed to be greater than for children with more calm dispositions. However, even if they never commit a crime, such behavior is antisocial and is thus damaging to children's success in life. Crime is the ultimate detrimental effect of televised violence, but certainly not the only one.

Columbia University in New York City conducted a research project that gives strong evidence of a relationship between heavy TV viewing and aggressive behavior. Researchers questioned mothers in a certain district of New York to find out: (1) what were their children's four favorite programs; (2) how many hours a week they watched; and (3) their children's attitudes and behavior in certain key areas. The results were tabulated statistically to show the relationship between a child's behavior and the kind of television programs he watched.

One of the behavior categories investigated was delinquency: the child who "does rash and dangerous things" and/or who is "in trouble with the police."[9] Children with high delinquency scores were found to consume more total violence on television than those with lower scores, and the most significant factor contributing to delinquency was the amount of time they spent in front of the TV. Children whose parents were on welfare were found to prefer a greater degree of violence in their TV programs, and a greater frequency of it than non-welfare children. Children from disadvantaged homes (in terms of family income, parents' education, etc.) watched the greatest amount of television violence. Significantly, children who preferred educational programs and who spent the least amount of time in front of the television set had the lowest aggression scores. These results seem to indicate, not that children from disadvantaged homes *will* watch more television violence, but that they *tend* to. Children from more advantaged homes who watch more violent television may react just as aggressively, and children from disadvantaged homes whose parents control their children's viewing will be less likely to react aggressively.

Parental involvement in children's television viewing is thus a key factor. This conclusion is strongly borne out in a study involving 800 children in grades four to six. The survey showed that in those homes in which the family's attitude toward violence and aggression was nebulous the child's violence score was higher.

Tolerance of Aggressive Behavior. One of the most significant effects of televised violence is an increased tolerance of aggressive behavior in others. This conclusion was strongly suggested in an interesting study conducted by Donald Drabman and Margaret Thomas at the Florida Technological University in Orlando.

Forty-four third- and fourth-grade children participated in the experiment, half boys and half girls.[10] The experimenter invited the children one at a time to play games with him. Each child was happy to cooperate. "But we've got just a little extra time," the experimenter told the child after they were out of the classroom "How would you like to look though the new trailer parked on the playground?"

In the trailer the child saw blocks, picture books, crayons, and other toys for kindergarten youngsters. A TV camera stood in one corner of the room. "A friend of mine and I are conducting an experiment with children," the researcher explained. "In just a few minutes he'll send two kindergartners in, and this television camera will pick up everything they do. We can watch them in another room."

The researcher then took the student into that other room for the games. The child saw the television screen from which he and the researcher could watch the activity in the kindergarten playroom. However, nobody had come to the playroom yet, so the researcher showed the child a Hopalong Cassidy film that contained considerable violence. After the films he checked the TV monitor again, and the kindergarten children still had not arrived. "Oh dear," he said, "I'm sure they'll be here any minute now. I've got to make a phone call. Would you watch this TV monitor while I'm gone? If the children get into any trouble, call me and I'll take care of them."

The researcher then left the room. Two minutes later

the student saw a small boy and girl enter the kindergarten room. Each child kept busy for a few minutes building his own block tower. Then the boy criticized the girl's tower, and she criticized his. The words became stronger, and the boy knocked the girl's tower over. The quarrel grew more intense, and suddenly the screen on the TV monitor went blank. The older student could still hear the two children quarreling, but he couldn't see them. The obvious conclusion was that the fighting had gotten so bad that the TV camera had been damaged.

The third- and fourth-grade children who participated in this experiment thought the incident they observed on the TV screen was happening live at the time they were in the room. In fact, the scene had been pre-recorded on video tape, and each child merely watched a replay. Two sets of forty-four children went through the same experiment, with one difference. One group saw the Hopalong Cassidy film just before the experimenter went to use the phone, and the other did not. The object of the experiment was to see whether the group that saw the film showed any greater tolerance of the kindergarten children's violence than those who did not see the violent film. According to the report, "even this brief exposure to the eight-minute Hopalong Cassidy film led to statistically different response times between the two groups. The children who saw the aggressive film took significantly longer to seek appropriate adult help than the children who did not see the film. There were no sex differences."[11]

The experiment was repeated two times with different sets of children. In the second experiment a modern detective film was used instead of the outdated

Hopalong Cassidy film. The results were even more significant. The third experiment involved forty fifth-grade children, and the results were the same. "These three studies provide strong evidence that continued exposure to TV violence is teaching children to accept aggression as a way of life," the experimenters concluded. "TV violence may be having the dual effect of exacerbating some children's violent behavior while at the same time teaching the rest to tolerate their aggression. A future society in which virtually all adults have been exposed to a continued deluge of violence since infancy could well be an unfortunate place to live."[12]

Distorted Reality. Television violence is not a realistic picture of normal life. For instance, how many killings will a child actually see in real life from birth through his graduation from high school? The average child won't even see one. Yet on TV he will see 18,000. He will see countless highly detailed incidents of robbery, arson, bombing, forgery, smuggling, beating, torture, and rape. None of these is he likely to see in real life, for life is not half filled with crime. But TV programming is. During 1975, so-called "action programs" (the industry's euphemism for programs heavy with violence) made up 54 percent of all prime-time programming. Nine out of ten Saturday morning children's programs averaged sixteen or more violent scenes per hour (including cartoons).

Several years ago, in a visit with a Houston policeman, I learned how easy it is to have a distorted notion of law enforcement. The officer I met happened to be a member of the crime control division of his department, and he attended the scenes of dozens of murders every year. He told me that almost invariably, murders are committed against either family members or close friends. I was surprised. But the officer explained that people generally kill in a fit of temper. We humans most easily become angry with those we are close to, whose behavior frustrates us. But on television murders are generally committed against strangers. Furthermore, real-life policemen almost never handle a gun, except during target practice. But it is a rare crime program that does not show the policeman on the draw at least once. And in real life, when violence does occur, it is often hideous, bloody, and sickening, a sharp contrast with the thrill of violence seen on TV.

Studies show that the impact of TV violence on people's view of life is not hypothetical. This is clearly seen in a survey conducted by George Gerbner and Larry Gross of the Annenberg School of Communications at the University of Pennsylvania in Philadelphia. The survey asked questions about people's concept of law enforcement. To the question, "What proportion of the population is employed in law enforcement?" Heavy TV viewers guessed 5 percent, and light viewers 1 percent. One percent is far closer to reality. To the question, "During any given week what are your chances of being involved in some type of violence?" heavy viewers responded one in ten, compared with the light viewers' one in a hundred. "Can most people be trusted?" Heavy viewers said, "You can't be too careful" in significantly larger numbers than light viewers, and women were the most likely to express distrust. A Detroit study showed that people's estimate of the danger in their neighborhoods had as much if not more to do with their exposure to televised violence as it did to actual crime statistics in their communities.

And perhaps most significantly, respondents under thirty years of age gave more consistently the "heavy viewer's" reponse than those over thirty. TV has been around about thirty years.[13]

Gerbner and Gross concluded the report on their study with this thoughtful comment: "A heightened sense of risk and insecurity . . . is more likely to increase acquiescence to and dependence upon established authority, and to legitimize its use of force, than it is to threaten the social order through occasional non-legitimized imitations. Risky for their perpetrators and costly for their victims, media-incited violence may be a price industrial culture exacts from some citizens for the general pacification of most others."[14] In plain English, is TV violence softening up the American population for a dictatorship?

Television is a powerful mental tool. People tend to go along with the basic assumptions of their society, and those assumptions are both created and reinforced as people communicate with each other. A medium that communicates with an entire population in its very living rooms is a powerful tool to mold public opinion, to instill and reinforce basic assumptions. What would be the consequence if a power were to come on the American scene that most citizens assumed to be good, and which was extremely popular, but which in fact was destructive of the freedoms we have enjoyed these hundreds of years? How large a role might television play in perpetrating a false sense of security on the public by inculcating certain false assumptions as real?

Is cartoon violence harmful? Cartoons have come in for their share of criticism because of violence. There are two kinds of TV cartoons: serious and comic. The serious cartoons, such as "Speed Racer" that was on the air during the early 1970s, are simply animated versions of regular crime dramas, with the added feature that the artists and programmers can enhance the action with scenes that would be impossible in real acting. For instance, a car can be given a sense of speed that it would never have in real life. A face can be drawn with a much more angry scowl than a real actor can put on, and because narration is tied to animation, the voices (including the violent tones of voice) can be accentuated much beyond what would be considered normal in real acting.

Comic cartoons also contain violence, but of a different sort. In comic cartoons characters can be smashed flat with a boulder, get up, stretch out, and keep going as though nothing had happened. There is not even the appearance of reality. The antics of Roadrunner as he tries to outwit the big bad coyote are funny. But cartoons such as "Popeye" are comic only in the sense that the characters are humorously drawn, and that they do things that are humanly impossible. The plots of these cartoons are serious, and generally malicious in their intent as well as in their violent action. Of more concern is children's obsession for cartoons. Even if every cartoon were nonviolent and harmless, preschoolers and children up to the age of ten would be happy to spend three hours a day watching the silly things, and there are lots better ways for children to spend their time than that.

TV actor Charles Bronson, whose chief qualification to fame is his ability to beat people up on the screen, says he is shocked at all the violence in children's cartoons: "I watched 'Road Runner' cartoons with my little girl. They dropped a rock on the coyote and flattened him—but he popped right up again."[15] Bronson calls this "frightening," because a youngster will grow up thinking he can hit people over the head with a hammer and they'll be all right. He contrasts this kind of violence with what he calls "clean violence" in his own "Death Wish" show: "When I shot a man he was shot—and that was the end of it. You didn't see the blood and guts running all over the place. You don't have to see that sort of thing. I object to a director exploiting blood. But to be shot cleanly by a bullet—that's not really overdoing it."

Bronson's opinion is debatable. Why should anybody shoot anybody? And as for "clean violence" versus the "dirty" kind, it is the dirty kind that happens in real life most often. Kids may be induced to violence by Bronson's so-called "clean" shooting because they *don't* see the blood and guts running all over the place. If they saw it, they might not imitate it. This is not an argument for showing the blood and guts. Why have it at all?

6
The Industry's View of Violence

Private and government scientists have conducted research for the past fifteen years that shows cigarette smoking to be detrimental to health. But to date the tobacco industry refuses to acknowledge the relationship unless forced to do so by law. Obviously, no industry is anxious to cut its financial lifeline. And the same is true of the television industry. A program's dollar value is measured by its place in the ratings. Violence is a proven way to achieve a high rating. The industry is naturally reluctant to concede the social harm of violent programs. Said one producer, whose police show attracted 40 million viewers, "If the show changed to a nonaction show, it would begin to fail; so violent action is necessary."[1] According to industry representatives, "violence is an economic imperative—the inescapable dictate of the commercial broadcast."[2]

The industry would like to ignore the social consequences of its violent programming. It plays down, and even opposes when it can, the serious research that links TV violence and aggressive behavior. An example of this was its response to a major government investigation of the effect of television on the American people. Called the *Surgeon General's Report* for short, the six-volume study includes twenty-three separate research projects and took about three years to complete. The TV industry had a major voice in the selection of the scientists who conducted the research and the committee that evaluated the findings. Seven leading American scientists involved in the study of TV violence were barred by the industry from participating in the government study because their previous research incriminated TV violence as a factor in aggressive behavior.

When the *Surgeon General's Report* was published in 1972, the industry claimed a victory for its point of view. *Broadcasting* magazine, an industry mouthpiece, headlined its first story on the report, "Violence on Air and in Life: No Clear Link."[3] One of the report's major recommendations was the creation of a "Violence Profile" to keep a continual eye on the degree of violence contained in future television programs. This Violence Profile drew especially heavy fire from the industry. Said Edith Efron in a three-part series in *TV Guide*, "You are now going to be presented with a 'Violence Index.' It will make most people yawn and tune in to 'Mission Impossible.' But it will throw others into a panic because they'll assume that there would be no 'Violence Index' without proof that TV violence is dangerous to young viewers. Be advised that the 'Violence Index' has only one real meaning: it is a nonsolution to a nonproved problem produced by a noninvestigation of a nonresolved controversy over a nondefined threat to a nonidentifiable people."[4] In other words, the problem does not exist.

Many columnists and reporters attacked the *Surgeon General's Report* as inconclusive, and with some justification. The TV industry's major role in its production can be likened to the defendant in a trial taking part in the decision of the jury. Many of the scientists who partcipated in the study criticized the report. Criticism centered on four points: (1) that the committee of twelve scientists who analyzed the research material was rigged in favor of the TV industry; (2) that the committee's 260-page report softened the research findings; (3) that the nineteen-page summary of the full report softened the findings even more; and (4) that the news media misread the summary and generally absolved TV violence of any significant effect on children."[5] There is no question that the report was an attempt to please all parties.

However, for all its ambiguities, it was sufficiently clear on the relationship between TV violence and aggressive behavior that thoughtful scientists acknowledged the relationship. After he left his government post, Surgeon General Jesse Steinfeld wrote, "These studies—and scores of similar ones—make it clear to me that the relationship between televised violence and antisocial behavior is sufficiently proved to warrant immediate remedial action. Indeed, the time has come to be blunt: We can no longer tolerate the present high level of televised violence that is put before children in American homes."[6]

Though it might wish the whole thing would blow away, the television industry knows it will not, and it defends its violent programming on several counts. One of its most frequently heard arguments is that violence is a part of American culture. It says that violent action and aggressive behavior won the country during its 300-year frontier history, and violent action is fundamental to the preservation of our freedom in time of war. Violent action is part of law enforcement, which insures the public peace. Aggressive behavior is often seen in competition between businesses in our economy. Violence is seen on the streets in large American cities, particularly in ghetto areas. Said one programmer, "Exposure to violence in childhood is not a bad idea. Maybe there should be a police show for kids. Ghetto children are exposed to violence unknown to other children. Because they have to live with it and it is so hateful, they might be less influenced by it than other kids who haven't encountered it."[7]

The industry claims violence on TV "tells it like it is." Even the Bible depicts violence, they say. Why can't we? In television the right side always wins. Such programs teach children our society's attitude toward violence and how to cope with it in their own lives. Violence may be part of the American culture, but television's crime dramas are not "telling it like it is." The industry's motive is dollars, not reality, and there is a vast amount of "over-kill" to push up the ratings. This does not teach children to cope with violence. It teaches them to commit it.

Another frequent argument advanced by the industry is that violence is cathartic to the viewer's emotions. Aristotle used this reasoning to defend violence in the Greek tragedies. Violent action on TV allows the viewer to vent his aggressive impulses vicariously, so the argument goes, rather than acting them out in real life. Watching someone else fight drains off one's own urge to fight. As one industry representative put it, "The little guy likes violence of this kind because he so seldom reacts effectively against the sources of his own irritations."[8] And, "Human culture is a thin shield superimposed over a violent core. It's better to crack it fictionally than to see it explode in the streets. Exposure to properly presented conflicts which result in violence acts is a therapeutic release for anger and self-hatred, which are present in almost everybody."[9] But it doesn't work that way. Violent drama is not a safety valve. It is more like the feeding of a fan-jet engine.

The industry also notes the fact that violence is relative. What seems violent to one person may not to another. Often, violence will be implied in a program but not shown, as when a character is shown dead or injured, and the viewer knows what happenend but the action itself happened off screen. Is this bad? To some, yes; to others, no. The public must depend on the judgment of programmers and censors who review each program before and after production. Obviously, not everyone will agree with the censor's judgment. The context of a show may determine whether the violence is justified, and the viewer's ability to perceive that context will determine whether he attributes to the violence the moral quality of right or wrong. It is true that people's judgments differ. Unfortunately, what the TV industry might judge as bad programming is in constant comparison with what is good business.

Sensitive to the criticism that its violent programming creates aggressive behavior, the industry notes that hereditary and environmental factors are often equally responsible. This is true. That's like the knife telling the razor it's sharp. When two factors are responsible for a problem, we don't use one to justify the other. We try to control both.

The industry's own code of ethics states a greater

concern for the public and its values than is evident on the screen. Several significant portions of the code, drawn up by the National Association of Broadcasters (NAB), are quoted below:

"It is the responsibility of television to bear constantly in mind that the audience is primarily a home audience, and consequently that television's relationship to the viewers is that between guest and host. . . . By law the television broadcaster is responsible for the programming of his station. He, however, is obligated to bring his positive responsibility for excellence and good taste in programming to bear upon all who have a hand in the production of programs, including networks, sponsors, producers of film and of live programs, advertising agencies and talent agencies.

"Television and all who participate in it are jointly accountable to the American public for respect for the special needs of children, for community responsibility, for the advancement of education and culture, for the acceptability of the program materials chosen for decency and decorum in production, and for propriety in advertising. This responsibility cannot be discharged by any given group of programs, but can be discharged only through the highest standards of respect for the American home, applied to every moment of every program presented by television.

"The presentation of techniques of crime in such detail as to invite imitation shall be avoided. . . . Violence and illicit sex shall not be presented in an attractive manner, nor to an extent such as will lead a child to believe that they play a greater part in life than they do."[10]

Critics insist that this code of ethics is simply a public

relations document that does not guide the actual production of programs.

Because of public and government pressure the industry agreed, beginning in September 1975, to set aside the two-hour slot from seven to nine p.m. (prime time) as "Family Hour." During this time material inappropriate for young children would not usually be shown, and advisories would be given to warn parents of programs both during and after Family Hour that might be harmful or offensive. The American public generally favored the Family Hour concept. Critics said it was only a "gentleman's agreement between Congress, the FCC, the networks, and the NAB to take the heat off all of them."[11] However, there has been a significant reduction of violence during these hours. The industry has tried.

There are several problems with the Family Hour concept. Nobody has defined just what might constitute "appropriate" family entertainment. Advisories about upcoming objectionable programs might lure kids into watching them anyway. Other children's programming on weekends and earlier in the afternoon were not affected. And violent programs during prime time were simply shifted to a later hour, when millions of children are still up staring at the tube. Perhaps most significantly, and predictably, Nielsen reported a 5 percent drop in the number of sets in use in the early evening.[12] And the trend is getting worse rather than better. Between March and October 1977 Nielsen reported a 3.4 percent drop each month in total viewing, both night and day.[13]

Few other American industries face the conflict between material and spiritual values that confronts network TV. It is not a conflict that will soon go away, and the solution as often as not will be in the individual Christian home rather than in the corporate television office.

7
Christianity and Violence

One of the simplest ways to solve the problem of violence on TV from a Christian point of view might seem to be to ask, "What programs would Jesus watch?" Whatever God says ought to be final. That sounds like a neat solution to a difficult problem. Unfortunately, God hasn't run a blue pencil through the bad programs in the *TV Guide*. It is still up to Christians to decide what programs "Jesus would watch." I seriously question whether He would tell us even if He were here. That's why He gave us minds.

Another simple solution to TV violence would be to switch off all the violent programs. That, too, is easier said than done. The TV industry correctly argues that what's violent to one person may not seem so to another. Two families might each decide to solve the violence problem by turning off all violence, yet one continue watching programs that the other turned off.

The strongest Christian answer to violence on television is to reach a general conclusion about violence from a biblical perspective and then to analyze TV violence in that framework.

Violence is contrary to the golden rule. It is contrary to God's original plan for man. God did not create violence in the Garden of Eden. He did not even intend that the mildest form of antisocial behavior should exist, let alone violence. It is still His plan that all men shall live at peace with one another, and someday He will put that plan into effect: "And God shall wipe away all tears from their eyes; and there shall be no more death, neither sorrow, nor crying, neither shall there be any more pain: for the former things are passed away" (Revelation 21:4). The society with that kind of social environment cannot have violence too.

Violence is a result of sin and pride. It began in heaven with Lucifer, who said, "I will be like the most High" (Isaiah 14:14). Lucifer's pride caused war to break out in heaven. Revelation 12:7. On this earth, Lucifer became Satan, the enemy of God and man. Violence broke out among men. Cain killed Abel. Within a few hundred years Satan had so perverted the minds and morals of the human race that the whole earth was filled with violence. Genesis 6:11. This is one of the chief reasons why God destroyed the world with a flood. The last days of earth's history will also be filled with violence. Jesus foretold wars and persecution. Matthew 24:6-9. In 2 Timothy 3:1-3 Paul described men in the last days as covetous, proud, false accusers, fierce, despisers of those that are good. All of these lead to violent action sooner or later.

Violence may be foreign to God's plan, but we do not live in God's perfect world. Violence is a fact of life that the Christian must cope with as much as the non-Christian. At times God's people themselves have used violence. Abraham got up an army to rescue Lot from the kings of Mesopotamia. God commanded the Israelites to destroy every living Amalekite. David killed

Goliath. The difference between violence in the Bible and that on television is motive. The Bible is a spiritual book whose chief object is to teach lessons about God and moral truth in the context of history. Violence is mentioned when it occurs. The television executive's motive is to earn a profit. He uses violence to catch the viewer's attention. To him, violence is not incidental. It is vital. Industry representatives admit this: "If the show changed to a nonaction show, it would begin to fail; so violent action is necessary."[1] "Violence is an economic imperative—the inescapable dictate of the commercial broadcasting system."[2]

Television executives argue that because violence is a fact of life it is justifiable on television. To a certain extent this is true. Some Christian films portray violence, too. Notable examples of this are Corrie Ten Boom's *The Hiding Place* and David Wilkerson's *The Cross and the Switchblade*. Violence is part of these stories. Telling them, or showing them on the screen, without violence would be unrealistic. But violence is not the objective of these films. Their producers did not include violence to get an audience. The violence in them is subordinate to larger themes of the stories.

Television violence, on the other hand, is portrayed for its own sake. An occasional overdose of violence in a program here and there might be excused on the grounds that what is excessive to one person is not to another. But when the schedule is overwhelmed with violence 365 days a year, year after year, something is wrong. And it is no longer just the Christian who objects. Secular society is alarmed too.

Violence on television is a form of entertainment. But it is not something to amuse the mind. It is serious business that the Christian ought to abhor. One of the detrimental effects of overexposure to violence is an increased tolerance for it. It can easily make the Christian insensitive to the biblical ideal. Violence may be a fact of life, but this does not excuse it or make it good, or justify parading it around for everyone to see.

Television crime drama presents violence as an almost exclusive method of solving problems. Many problem situations that crime drama builds up are realistic enough, but there are other ways to solve them than violence. Unfortunately, television producers are not looking for those other ways, that don't make money. But the Christian must seek all possible solutions to problems other than the violent ones.

Jesus said, "Ye shall know the truth, and the truth shall make you free" (John 8:32). Many people think this means having a correct doctrine, but it applies equally well to one's view of life. A paranoid person sees the same events as the mentally healthy person, but he misinterprets them. An environment dominated by a paranoid person's mentality is oppressive, filled with suspicion and false accusations about the intentions of others. A correct interpretation of the events occurring throughout the day is essential to a happy, free life. Overexposure to violence on television can create a false sense of anxiety about the real world, thus casting a shadow over the happy, free life that God planned the Christian should have.

Research shows that violence has a much greater detrimental effect in homes in which the family's attitude to violence and aggression is nebulous. This is why it is important for Christians to have a clear biblical understanding of violence. In principle, the Christian con-

dems all violence as evil. In reality, he must cope with it. The following questions can help the Christian to reach a satisfactory relationship to the violence and aggression that he must live with:
1. Am I preoccupied with it?
2. Am I insensitive to its evil?
3. Do I entertain myself with it?
4. Do I use it as a major way to solve my own problems?
5. Is it warping my realistic view of life?

These five questions can go a long way toward helping to evaluate which programs to watch on television and which ones to turn off.

8

Television and Sex

In 1975 the television industry finally curtailed violence during prime time. The result was a 5 percent drop in the viewing audience. In 1977 the industry turned to a new theme to attract viewers: sex during prime time. In an article headlined, "More Sex, Less Violence: TV's New Pitch," *U.S. News and World Report* said, "Public complaints about too much mayhem on television have paid off—much of the gore is being eliminated. But what is replacing it is proving to be at least as controversial.... As the new TV season unfolds (1977-78), it is clear that a major shift in emphasis is underway in many programs—away from violence and towards sex. A variety of old taboos, from impotence to homosexuality, will be treated with a candor that already has many critics seething and local station managers worried about repercussions."[1]

One of the most widely criticized programs is ABC's "Soap." The program includes a gay teenager who wants a sex change operation from boy to girl, a husband who can't get interested in women and another who can't keep his hands off, an adolescent fascinated with pornograpy, and a mother and a daughter who have bedroom dates with the same man. Till the censors got hold of it, one episode plotted the seduction of a Catholic priest in church, followed by another with an exorcism for the illegitimate baby. Said *Newsweek*'s Harry Waters, "'Soap' promises to be the most controversial network series of the coming season, a show so saturated with sex that it could replace violence as the PTA's Video Enemy No. 1."[2]

Sex is one of the physical drives that, like eating, combines with pleasure. Anyone who spends two minutes scanning the magazine rack at a drug store will discover that Americans are fascinated with it. Contemporary magazines feature a quick front-cover review of the most attractive topics inside. It's a rare cover that doesn't include the word "sex" among the listings. Editors refuse to whistle the same tune twice. An author treating a familiar topic must give it a new twist if he expects the editor to buy it. A review of the sex articles in a dozen popular magazines is an exercise in variety on a worn-out theme.

Television has torn a page out of the magazine industry's manual and put it on the screen for the same reason: to see if it would sell. Hook the viewer. Push up the ratings. Keep the dollars rolling in from advertisers. As with violence, the industry's concern is money, not morality. "'Soap' needs its mouth washed out," said one station manager. "It's not a new frontier, it's a new sewer."[3] But *Newsweek* notes that "the reaction is more positive among advertising folk, who sense a ratings smash. 'Salaciousness has its rewards,' shrugs Bruce Cox, TV programming director at Compton Advertising. 'A lot of people are going to jump on this bandwagon.' ... In short, absolutely nothing is 'too weird' for ABC—as long as the ratings are right."[4]

"ABC's treatment of sex is also slanted in favor of the young," said *Time* magazine's Frank Rich. "The Tuesday night sitcoms are a giddy celebration of post-pubescent horniness (teenage sex). . . . 'Three's Company' spend(s) so much time trying to turn their platonic *ménage à trois* (love triangle) into an orgy that the show has the dizzy ambience of a junior high coed slumber party. Adults do not have nearly as much fun. . . . The only sexual state funnier than menopause is homosexuality."[5]

The networks argue that their programs only reflect changing social attitudes, that most programming is determined by extensive surveys showing what viewers want. "Television must strike the delicate balance between following public taste and leading it by offering new forms and styles of entertainment," said NBC's president, Herbert S. Schlosser. "We do not seek through entertainment to create a new morality. But we must serve the millions of viewers who want at least part of their entertainment to relate to experience of the real world with which they can identify. In keeping pace with the times, we do not intend to leap too far ahead of what viewers will accept, but we cannot lag so far behind that they leave us and turn elsewhere."[6]

Victorian Christians may be horrified at sex, but the Bible isn't. One of the most beautiful passages in literature is the Song of Solomon, a poem about two lovers. Some scholars interpret the poem as a type of the Christian's love for Christ, and the parallel is appropriate. But in its historical setting the poem is a romance, the expression of affection between a man and a woman who are genuinely in love. Whether the events occurred exactly as described is beside the point. There can be no doubt that they reflect the attitudes and the customs prevalent among Jewish people at the time the book was written. Good taste is maintained throughout the poem, yet there is no prudishness, no embarrassment over the fact that two people love each other and want to be close together physically as well as spiritually.

At the same time, the Bible insists on certain standards of sexual conduct. The seventh commandment specifically forbids adultery, the sexual union of a married person with someone other than his spouse. In a broader sense it forbids any form of sexual promiscuity, and other Bible passages clarify what these are: homosexuality, incest, intercourse with animals, etc. (see Leviticus 18:6-18; Romans 1:26; 1 Corinthians 5:1-5). Paul speaks frequently of "the flesh" and the "lusts of the flesh" in Romans 8:5-8 and Galatians 5:16, 17. Some Christians assume that "the flesh" means sex—all sex. However, Paul did not condemn sex within marriage. He encouraged it: "Let each man have his own wife and each woman her own husband. The husband must give the wife what is due to her, and the wife equally must give the husband his due. . . . Do not deny yourselves to one another" (1 Corinthians 7:2-5, *The New English Bible*).

It is fashionable today to joke about biblical morality. But God had a reason for the standards He gave. The Song of Solomon presents attitudes about physical and spiritual love in an ideal setting. There would be fewer divorces today if husbands and wives felt about each other the way the two lovers felt in the Song of Solomon. The purpose of God's standards of sexual morality was not to inhibit sex but to preserve its beauty; not to make it less happy but more happy.

The new prime-time sex comedies are not pornographic. They do not show explicit sex scenes, though some may come close to it. The problem from a Christian perspective is that they make light of something very serious. Sex is funny on "Soap." But it is not in real life. Marital stability depends, among other things, on a satisfactory sexual adjustment and that is serious, not funny. There are programs on TV in which sex is treated with warmth and good taste, in which an embrace or a kiss occurs in a context of genuine affection between a man and a woman. These can lead all of us, adults as well as children, to better sexual adjustment. But sex must not be portrayed day after day as a joke. Susan Franzblau has stated it well: "On TV it tends to be all right to laugh about sex, but not all right to take it seriously as a natural part of a loving relationship. . . . Our concerns about sex are serious and as persistent as our sexual lives. In a sense, TV seems to be afraid to give more meaning to an area of deep concern. If we learn from TV, is there not some way we can treat these matters as we treat our other concerns? Is there not some way our children can have the opportunity to learn in an honest, direct way about a most important part of their lives? If TV reflects things to come, do we honestly want TV to teach us to laugh at everything having to do with sex?"[7]

NBC president Herbert Schlosser said that TV serves "the millions of viewers who want at least part of their entertainment to relate to experience of the real world with which they can identify." Do most people joke at home about sex? An occasional bit of humor comes out spontaneously in every marriage, or it should. But do

64

we continually laugh about sex and all sorts of sexual irregularities?

In some homes sex is the last thing laughed at. It is a point of bitter contention between husband and wife. Victorian prudishness is unrealistic, and our society is well on its way to being relieved of that. But current sex comedies are as unrealistic on the other side as Victorianism is in its extreme. Neither is the right attitude toward sex.

Fortunately, television is not a sex wasteland. Sex is a home relationship, and there are several programs that portray warm home relationships in an interesting, often dramatic format. "The Waltons," "Little House on the Prairie," "The Brady Bunch," and "Family Affair" portray family closeness, enthusiasm, and loyalty the way it ought to be. Sexual scenes—embracing, holding hands, kissing—in this context help develop attitudes in both children and adults that will make our lives happier, richer, and fuller.

An objection to "Little House on the Prairie" and "The Waltons" is that they are cast in a different age, 50 and 100 years ago. Are their values useful in the latter half of the twentieth century? I believe we need more programs portraying their values in a contemporary setting.

Some may argue that programs like this are as unrealistic as the comedies that laugh at sex, that quarreling and bitterness are a lot more realistic than idealized home life. But these programs don't make life out to be a paradise. Feelings get hurt and people get angry. Maybe they choose the right way to solve problems more often than the average person does in real life. There is something to be said for presenting healthy problem-solving methods on TV whether they happen to be common in society or not. Most people would be a lot happier if they learned them. Television is performing a valuable service to society in scheduling these programs and others like them.

The Christian condemns all violence in principle, recognizing that he must cope with it in reality. Something of the opposite is true of sex. The Christian approves of sex in principle, and attempts to grow in his relationship to it in reality. The following questions can help the Christian to choose television programs to help him or her achive that goal:

1. Does the program treat sex like a joke?
2. Does it exploit sex for entertainment and thrills?
3. Does it make me insensitive to the seriousness and sacredness of sex?
4. Does it present sex as a healthy aspect of a happy marriage?

Some Christians object to any demonstration of affection on the screen. But if a program adheres to the principles of biblical morality and general modesty, affection on the screen can benefit everyone, including children.

9
The Positive Effects of Television

Most studies on the impact of television investigate its negative effects, with violence heading the list. This is understandable, considering that by the early 1960s 60 percent of prime-time programming was devoted to violence-saturated adventure programs.[1] However, the heavy concentration of research on TV's negative impact to the exclusion of its positive effects is an injustice to both television as a medium of communication and to the television industry that puts forth such great technical effort each year to produce high quality programming.

Rita Poulos, a social scientist engaged in TV research, notes that "evidence of a causal link between viewing televised violence and later aggressive behavior by children . . . reasonably leads to the expectation that televised *positive* social examples might influence young viewers in salutary ways. Considering the importance of this possibility for the socialization of the young, it is striking that so little is known about the potentially positive influence of the medium."[2]

Several church groups recently united to produce three thirty-second spots for television that emphasized the value of resolving conflicts peacefully. In one of these spots, a boy and a girl run for a swing, reach it at the same time, and begin quarreling over who will go first. At that instant the motion freezes and a voice from off the screen says, "What would you do?" One of the children suggests taking turns, and the screen then shows them swinging one at a time. The off-screen voice says, "There are lots of things you can do when two people want the same thing. One is to take turns. And that's a good one."[3]

Hundreds of television stations around the nation donated time to show this spot announcement and the other two like it. The networks also used the announcements repeatedly during their children's viewing hours. A research team and a production company cooperated in the creation of these spots. They were particularly careful to produce a message that children could understand easily, that would attract attention, and that children would use as a guide for their own behavior.

In a test run of "The Swing" along with two regular television commercials, the children's average comprehension of "The Swing" was 93 percent, compared with 57 percent and 67 percent for the commercials. Researchers trained videocameras on children watching the spot to test its ability to capture attention. Children showed significantly greater attention to the spot announcement than to the regular commercials. To test whether children adopted the message of "The Swing" for their own behavior, researchers devised a game that involved two children pushing a special button to get points. Several teams of children were tested, some teams seeing only "The Swing" prior to playing the game and others seeing only regular commercials. The researchers reported that "children who had seen "The Swing" were two to three times more likely to cooperate than those who had not."[4]

Producing spots like this is not simple. The picture and the acting must be equal to that on regular programming or the message will appear cheap to the children, and thus of less importance to their own lives. The situation must be one that children will recognize instantly and that will display a high level of action in working out a solution to the problem. To present all this in a way that will grab children's attention and motivate their behavior requires the best equipment and the best writers, actors, and producers. Thousands of dollars go into the production of one thirty-second spot announcement. One can only speculate as to the results if children saw several such spot announcements each day on television.

Fortunately, much has been done in the past thirty years to produce entire programs for children that inspire positive social action. "The Wonderful World of Disney," "Lassie," "Little House on the Prairie," "The Brady Bunch," and similar programs depict positive social lessons week after week. Several have been developed to teach both learning skills and pro-social behavior to young children. Among these are "Sesame Street," "Mister Rogers' Neighborhood," "The Electric Company," and "Zoom." Nature pictures include ABC's "Animals, Animals, Animals;" CBS's "Animal World," and "Wild Kingdom." "Wonderful World of Disney" also features many animal pictures.

Comedies may be a waste of time, but they are not generally violent, and many of them do not contain sex innuendos. Some even make a stab at teaching a pro-social lesson now and then. Among the more harmless comedies are "Andy Griffith," "I Love Lucy," "Dick Van Dyke," and "Gilligan's Island," though if plain stupidity be ojectionable all the latter would certainly have to be struck from the list along with some episodes of "Lucy." "Lucy" is the longest lasting and the most loved of all American comedy programs.

Cartoons draw mixed opinions, but at their worst they are better for children than crime dramas and sex-saturated comedies. "The Flintstones" attracts a wide young audience. Whatever its demerits (sex-stereotyping, foolishness, etc.) it is not violent or sexually suggestive. Among positive television programs that do not fall into any other category mentioned are "Emergency," "Wide World of Sports," and "Lawrence Welk." And there are many, many others. Television is not a complete wasteland of violence, crime, and sex.

A number of studies have determined that children's attitudes and behavior can be affected by positive programs. Thirty-five first graders —boys and girls near-equally divided— from a predominantly white, middle-class public school were shown pro-social and neutral "Lassie" films which had appeared on regular television broadcasts. The children were divided into two groups. One group saw a film in which a boy risked his life to rescue one of Lassie's puppies that had fallen into a mine shaft. The other group saw the neutral film, which showed the same boy attempting to get out of violin lessons. A third group of children viewed a comedy program, "The Brady Bunch." The children were tested one at a time. They had to choose between earning points toward a prize (the more points the better the prize) by punching one button or by helping some puppies in a nearby kennel by punching another button that would call the experimenter, who was out of the room. The children heard the increasingly frantic barking from the kennel through an intercommunication system. The children who saw the pro-social "Lassie" program "helped" the puppies in the kennel significantly more than those who saw the neutral "Lassie" or "The Brady Bunch." No significant difference occurred between the responses of children who saw the neutral programs.[5]

A Canadian research group conducted an experiment to determine the impact of television on the racial attitudes of 205 preschool, upper middle-class children from white, English-speaking homes. Experimenters inserted a series of racially significant episodes into the Canadian Broadcasting Corporation's version of "Sesame Street." Some showed nonwhite (black, Indian, Oriental, etc.) and French Canadian children in nonintegrated settings while others showed English-speaking children playing with children of other ethnic groups. In each case, ethnic children were presented positively. Several episodes were used to show each ethnic group in both integrated and nonintegrated settings. A control group viewed "Sesame Street" without ethnic episodes. After the children viewed "Sesame Street" programs, researchers approached each child with photographs of scenes from the TV inserts. Some showed white, English-speaking children. Others showed children of various races. Each child was asked to choose which group of children he would like to play with the next day at the nursery school.

Seventy-one percent of the children who viewed the

racially significant episodes expressed a desire to play with children of other ethnic groups the following day, compared to only 33 percent of the children in the control group who saw the "Sesame Street" programs with no inserts.

The research team concluded that "minimal television exposure produced very clear-cut short-term attitude change toward televised children of other racial and ethnic groups. Further research should examine... long-term attitude change."[6]

Television is a powerful educational medium. Rightly used, it could teach children many positive lessons about life. Experiments mentioned in this chapter give some idea of the possibilities. If a single exposure to positive episodes influences children's attitudes and behavior, what might be the long-range effect of positive programs, reinforcing specific lessons day after day? And how might this affect the crime rate in our country if it were shown exclusively, without competing violent and sexually suggestive programs? Experimentation already done suggests that there would be a very noticeable difference. Proper use of the channel selector and the on-off button can produce the same results on an individual basis as might be obtained nationwide if all programming were positive.

Television has the power to supplement God's instruction to "repeat them [My commandments] to your sons, and speak of them indoors and out of doors, when you lie down and when you rise" (Deuteronomy 6:7, *The New English Bible*). Whatever blame we may cast for the negative effect of violence and sex on television, we must not forget to express appreciation for the many positive programs.

10
Television and the School

American educators are worried. Scholastic achievement of the nation's young people has declined for 15 years. The facts justify the concern.

- Entering college freshmen are required to take an aptitude test to determine their fitness for higher education, one of the most common of which is the Scholastic Aptitude Test. The verbal score (ability to use language) average was 478 nationwide in 1963. Fifteen years later, by mid-1977, that score had fallen by more than 10 percent, to 429. The math score fell from 502 to 470, a drop of 6.5 percent. The American College Testing exam shows a similar decline in results.
- Tests showed that essays of thirteen- and seventeen-year-olds in 1975 were far more awkward, incoherent, and disorganized than were similar essays written by students in 1969.
- The University of California at Berkeley takes the top 12.5 percent of high school graduates, yet 1974 saw nearly half the freshman class in remedial English.
- The proportion of freshmen failing English placement examinations at Temple University in Philadelphia increased by more than 50 percent between 1968 and 1975.

- The Civil Service Commission recently doubled its writing instruction program in order to develop adequate government employees.
- Businessmen report increasing difficulty in finding secretaries and clerks who can write and spell the English language correctly.[1]

Several factors appear to have caused this decline in scholastic ability of American youth, particularly their inability to write: A growing proportion of college applicants from disadvantaged backgrounds; an increase in elective courses, which reduces the number of basic required courses; a greater emphasis on individual "creativity" among students to the detriment of solid learning; less firm discipline by parents and teachers in requiring mastery of basic skills; the growing divorce rate and consequent family instability; and the youth unrest of the 1960s and 1970s.

Television has also received its share of the blame. The question in this chapter is, "What factors about television might contribute to a decrease in children's scholastic ability?"

Television is entertaining. School is hard work. Given a choice, the average youngster will drift toward the entertainment rather than the work. Television does not require the motivation to success that school does. The modern emphasis in learning is to make it fun. Students learn more quickly, we are told, when they enjoy the process. It is true that we learn better when we want to learn. But there is a difference between the fun of work and the fun of entertainment. If by making school fun we mean making it entertaining, then we have robbed the student of the pleasure of success through hard work. Students entertained by TV several hours a day will not be as interested in their education as those required to do chores and homework. Learning really is not hard for children. If their natural inquisitiveness at age two is not stymied by TV, it will lead naturally to fun and success through hard work. But the entertainment fun of TV is not the kind of learning that kids can grow on.

There is nothing so close to doing nothing as sitting in front of a TV. All the viewer has to do is sit there and soak up the information. Reading, on the other hand, requires concentration. Words will not get into the reader's mind without effort. Furthermore, reading requires learning to read. That takes time and hard work.

Reading forms a visual image of abstract ideas in the mind: the words on the page, the charts and diagrams and the illustrations. Television is also a visual medium, but the words are spoken. One of the chief characteristics that distinguishes man from the animal is man's ability to understand abstract ideas. But abstract ideas cannot be depicted on the screen in pictures. Yet a student can pore over a book by the hour till he learns his lesson. This kind of disciplined study builds the mind, but it is this very study that television induces children to avoid.

The average American child of school age watches television three to four hours a day, and some as much as six hours a day. By the time he graduates from high school the average American child will have spent 15,000 hours watching TV and only 11,000 hours in actual classroom instruction. This in itself should tell us something about why children are slipping in classroom achievement. Television came into its own in the 1950s. By the end of the decade 86 percent of all U.S.

homes had at least one set. Predictably, within five years scholastic achievement tests began to show the results of the wasted time, and it has been getting worse ever since.

But there is more to this massive exposure to television than wasted time. I can best illustrate the point with an experience I had recently. During an intensive research project I purchased a book and spent a whole day reading. It was a rather technical book and somewhat out of my field of training. However, I wanted to understand it. I focused my attention, and found that I understood it quite well. Toward the end of the day, though, the material became difficult to understand. I concluded that I had finally gotten in "over my head," that the increasing complexity of the subject in the latter half of the book went beyond my ability to understand. I felt tired, so I put the book aside and busied myself with other affairs. The next day I picked up the book and read again the chapter that had seemed so difficult the evening before. To my surprise I found that it was not any worse than the material in the first part of the book. After a day's exposure, my mind became saturated. It needed a rest.

Television stimulates the mind too. Werner Halpern, clinical assistant professor of psychiatry at the University of Rochester in New York, has done a study on the effects of overstimulation of children's minds by television.[2] Halpern found that overstimulation can cause hyperactivity. He found also that it can impair learning through sensory overload. A youngster who comes home from a day of mental stimulation at school and sits down to two or three hours of cartoons and comedies will have saturated his brain for that day. No wonder he is not interested in homework that evening. His mind needs to spend those hours after school playing and working about the house, preferably outside. Some youngsters watch TV till ten or eleven at night. Even a night's rest is not enough to refresh the mind subjected to that kind of sensory barrage, and the student walks into the classroom the next morning already drained. No wonder junior is not interested in school.

The most significant area in which scholastic achievement has dropped is in the ability to write. Educators attribute this to a decrease in the volume of children's reading. "Writing is book-talk," says Dr. Ramon Veal, associate professor of language education at the University of Georgia. "You learn book-talk by reading."[3] Educators suggest that the reason children cannot read and write is because of the simplistic spoken style of television to which America's youth have been exposed the past two decades. In an article, "Why Johnny Can't Write," *Newsweek's* Merrill Sheils said, "No one has yet produced a thorough study of the effect of TV on a generation of students raised in its glare, but on at least two points most language experts agree: time spent watching television is time that might otherwise be devoted to reading; and the passiveness of the viewing . . . seems to have a markedly bad effect on a child's active pursuit of written skills."[4] And E. B. White, one of America's leading writers, says point blank that "short of throwing away all the television sets, I really don't know what we can do about writing."[5]

The drop in America's scholastic achievement is one problem for which the television industry is not largely responsible. Morals is not the point. The industry has committed itself to maintaining a schedule during the waking hours of the day. Be the programming 100 percent pure, if people can't turn their sets off when they should, the industry can't be blamed.

And there is hope for the future on at least two counts. By early 1978 a new viewing trend had became clear: Americans were spending less time in front of the tube. Daytime viewing was down 8 percent from the previous season and prime-time viewing was down 3 percent. Reasons for the trend range from more working women to smaller families to the networks' recent trend to change schedules too much, leaving viewers confused. Haynes Johnson of the *Washington Post* has a suggestion of his own: "I'll offer a seat-of-the-pants guess why so many viewers appear to be turning on and off—or not turning on at all: They have managed to find something better to do with their time."[6] If Johnson is right, the schools can start cheering. Reading is one of the better things children and young people could find to do with their time.

The second positive note is that television *can* contribute to reading and learning, if it is used right. Educational programs such as "Sesame Street" and the "Electric Company" are geared specifically to help young children learn reading and mathematics skills. Research over the past few years shows that the programs do help children, including the disadvantaged, to acquire basic skills.[7] Mothers in New York's Bedford-Stuyvesant and East Harlem districts and in Chicago credit the programs with helping their children to read and count better, thus preparing them to do better in school.[8]

Several experiments have combined television with reading for older children. Dr. Michael McAndrews, a reading instructor in the Philadelphia school system, uses regularly scheduled network dramas and comedies to encourage junior and senior high school students to read. He arranged with the ABC television network to have the entire script of the January 11 and 12, 1976, "Eleanor and Franklin" program printed in the *Philadelphia Inquirer*. The script appeared in the paper of January 9. That day's circulation of the newspaper jumped from the normal 410,000 to 550,000. An estimated 84 percent of the students involved in the experimental program watched the show while following along in the printed script. McAndrew checked with all thirty bookstores in Philadelphia a few days later and found that all but two had sold out their large stocks of the 931-page book on which the TV program was based. The kids were reading, and TV turned the trick. Several thousand other school systems around the country are trying similar reading experiments.[9]

"Instead of considering television an anti-education monster, most educators today accept it as an integral part of a child's life and are searching for ways to incorporate its drawing power into instructional programs," say Anne Adams and Cathy Harrison, reading specialists in Durham and Fayetteville, North Carolina.[10] And why not? Americans are famous for their ability to tackle a problem and solve it. Why not this one? Our intellectual survival is at stake.

11

Television and You

I still remember the summer I was 10. That was 1947 and nobody had TV back then. Or air conditioning. The days were hot and boring. My sister and I sought out our mother in the sewing room one afternoon. "Mamma," we groaned, "what can we do?"

Mamma ran her needle through the cloth two or three times before she answered. "Go outside and play," she said.

"But we've played everything we know," we protested. "Tell us what to do."

A couple of stitches later she looked up again. "Find something to do," she said.

I suppose modern educators would accuse my mother of neglecting her children's developing minds. What an opportunity to think up ways to channel our interests into arts and crafts, lessons in cooking, or some new game. Perhaps. But I think my mother's way was best. By refusing to exercise her own imagination she forced us to exercise ours.

That is one of the chief problems with TV. It spoon feeds. Activity is never a problem with kids, because canned entertainment is always available at the push of a button. Regrettably, today's kid never gets bored. He never has to figure out for himself what to do. Keeping his mind busy is never *his* problem. For all the hue and cry over violence and sex, I'm impressed that some of TV's most unfortunate sins go unnoticed. How much creativity is stifled? How much time is wasted? How much brain power is killed by passive attention?

There is one other question even more vital to the Christian.

Establishing a relationship with Christ is the most important priority in the Christian's life. Man is a sinner by nature, and Christ is the only one who can change that. "If any man be in Christ, he is a new creature" (2 Corinthians 5:17). Christians call this change the new birth. This experience changes the Christian's view of himself. If he is criticized, for instance, he may smile because he does not feel threatened, or if he feels threatened and reacts in an unchristian way he will recognize his mistake and apologize for it. His ultimate goal is to develop a calm trust in God that keeps his emotions above selfish concern over *his* rights, *his* dignity, and *his* way of doing things.

Television can work against this goal in two ways. First, television models, even in programs considered by secular standards as healthy, often portray values and solutions to problems that are out of harmony with Christian standards. Soap operas that focus on marriage problems, for instance, may suggest solutions that violate the seventh commandment. Do we want our families exposed, day after day, to programming that is "OK," except that it continually instills non-Christian values and solutions to problems? What do quiz and other game programs that give away expensive prizes teach the Christian about the value of things? What do the comedies tell him he should laugh at? The answer may not in every case be to turn off the program but the Christian should analyze programs that differ with his biblical values rather than passively absorb them for what they are worth.

Time is the second significant factor to the born-again Christian. Establishing a relationship with Christ means learning to know Him as a friend. This is the way Christians receive the new birth. Earthly friendships take time. Lovers spend hours—whole days—courting each other before they get married. The Christian must determine to provide the time to keep his friendship with Christ alive. Taking time for Christ is so important that God set aside one whole day in seven for that purpose.

There is no way a person can spend several hours a day watching television, keep up with other responsibilities of life, and spend time with Christ necessary to maintain a healthy Christian experience. Christians used to argue that they did not have time in the busy day for Bible study and prayer. Television disproved that myth. We have time for the things we want. The only reason we do not have time for Christ is that we have not made up our minds that He is that important. TV is an idol that will cost some people eternal life.

The first step toward controlling television is a firm decision that it shall be controlled. Once that is settled, there are two options: getting rid of the TV, or keeping it and choosing the programs. Getting rid of the TV is the most painful to begin with, but in the end it is the easiest. Short of spending the money for another set, there is no way to go back on the resolution. Many people who decide to keep the TV and choose the programs discover their enthusiasm waning, and soon they are back at the old routine. However, some Christian families do succeed admirably in controlling their television.

When children are very young, parents can choose their programs for them, and the children will accept it. As they grow older, the children have ideas of their own about what to watch and when, and conflicts arise. Fortunately, the English language has provided a very convenient tool for parents to settle these conflicts. It's fast, and it's final. It's the word *no*. Nothing provokes a child to argue faster than an indecisive parent. And nothing settles arguments faster than a parent who takes a position and refuses to budge. Parents must be in charge of the atmosphere of the home, and their children's upset feelings must not be allowed to move them one inch.

Saying No, however, is not the parent's only responsibility. He must also train his child to say No to himself. The parent must teach his child to make decisions based on principle. Parents ought to include their children in the decision about TV from the time the children are about eight years old. Even younger than that would be appropriate, simply to get the children in the habit of choosing programs according to principle. But by the age of eight it is psychologically wise to let children feel that they are a part of the decision-making team.

If a family viewing pattern has been established for several years, and there is a fair amount of agreement between parent and child over the principles for choosing programs, then, between the ages of fifteen and twenty the conflict will probably be minimal.

But what should the Christian parent do who finds himself irreconcilably in conflict with an older teenager over what programs to watch or how much time to spend watching? Ask the teenager to postpone watching the program till you have had time to talk about it, and then be sure to make time before the next episode is scheduled. A council that includes all family members is especially valuable when it can be arranged. In the discussion, state frankly to the teenager the reasons for preferring that he not watch a particular program. However, if the teenager absolutely refuses to accept the parents' point of view about an objectionable program, tell him he cannot watch it in the home. Control of the house has been given to the parents, and they have a right at all times to control the atmosphere of the home. At some future time the child may have children, and at that time control of the home atmosphere will pass into his hands.

Teenagers ought to respect their parents' principles about TV programs. But some parents are overbearing, and/or some teenagers are extemely determined to have their own way. Some parents may feel that evil is accomplished by letting a determined teenager watch his own programs, no matter how bad the parents may think them to be, than by creating a permanent storm in the house. A six-year-old can be spanked and sent to his room, but that is not the way to handle a TV conflict with a sixteen-year-old. Teenagers have a keen sense of fairness, and most of them will cooperate with a plan that respects their own rights and those of the rest of the family.

Another problem is TV addiction. The TV addict watches television the way the alcoholic drinks wine—

compulsively. He will snap off the set to attend his mother's funeral (grudgingly), but normally when his program is on, he is glued to the tube. And he has programs all day long, or during his nonbusiness hours till bedtime, that he just *has* to see. It is an escape from reality. It is easier to drown out conflict, guilt, or a sense of failure than it is to face it and do something about it. Television can create its own dependency. A child who is afraid to play with other children may sit down and watch a TV program instead. He uses it to avoid handling his problem. And one time won't hurt anything. But it relieves the pain, so the next time he tries it again; and again and again. Soon, instead of stiffening his backbone and handling his problem, he has learned to escape into a fantasy world that temporarily blots it out. He begins to handle other emotional problems the same way, and he is on the way to a full-blown case of TV addiction. After a year his problems are harder to face, and after ten years he may find them impossible. TV addiction is complete.

The surgeon does not cut out cancer a piece at a time. He takes the whole tumor. The TV addict needs radical surgery, too. Cold turkey. Getting rid of the set is the only way. Trying to control the viewing is, for the TV addict, like the alcoholic trying to control his drinking.

The addict will find that TV withdrawal has certain definite symptoms. "I've talked to literally hundreds of parents who've withdrawn their children from TV," says Dr. Gordon Livingston, a child psychiatrist in Washington, D.C. "Almost uniformly they report agitation, inability to fill time, and a high level of irritability,"[1] Adults usually experience the same symptoms. It is especially important for the person who plans a clean break with TV to understand the symptoms he can expect. It helps just to know that what is happening is normal, and that in time it will go away. Also, the person who knows ahead of time what to expect can plan activities that will minimize symptoms.

Boredom is one of the most common symptoms. Most people have some spare time, and using it constructively takes planning. Some people are TV addicts because they have not planned their lives. Escaping from this kind of TV addiction is often simply a matter of initiating the plans. Fill the hours with other activities. And be sure they are activities you find interesting. Do you enjoy Monopoly, Scrabble, or checkers? Buy a set or a favorite game. Invite friends over to dinner one evening during the week. Go out to supper. Get involved in PTA, the local Pathfinder club, or other church activity. Attend the city council. Take in a concert if you are the concert kind.

Irritability is another symptom of TV withdrawal, and that has to do with the nerves. Nerves are a part of the physical organism, and willpower is not the only way to calm them. One of the best ways to reduce tension is exercise. Try jogging. Swimming or cycling work just as well for those who prefer them. Nature has a regular pep pill built right into your food—Vitamin B. A switch to whole-grain bread can help you feel better. Oxygen is another of nature's "pepper-uppers," which is one reason why exercise helps. It makes you breathe deeper. Fresh air in your bedroom at night can also make the difference between feeling dead or alive the next morning. Open the window a couple of inches and turn the electric blanket up a notch. And if you are real brave, try ending your shower each morning with half a minute of cold water. For anyone interested in working off irritability and tension, *that works*!

Remember that nature also has its nerve irritants: caffeine, nicotine, alcohol, and too much sugar among others. People who cut these out of their diet often report a definite psychological boost. Try switching from sugarcoated cereal in the morning to Wheaties, and cut deserts at lunch and dinner in half. Your dentist will notice the difference too!

It has become quite fashionable to lay all the blame for children's aggression on violent TV programs. This is a factor, as we have seen. The television industry, however, has correctly pointed out that other factors are equally to blame, and perhaps more so. An imbalanced diet can make a child irritable and aggressive. So can unwise methods of discipline—too much or not enough, or either kind in the wrong way. Tension between parents always upsets children. If you are concerned about aggressive behavior in your child, check the TV programs he watches, but do not stop there. Rarely is TV the only cause, or the only cure.

Handling a child's addiction requires the parents' firm decision first. Children whose excessive television is suddenly restricted often become very agitated and demanding, but if parents persist, the children will adjust. A firm *no* cuts through a lot of nagging. Within a week or two the irritability should decrease noticeably. At first, parents should plan activities to busy children's minds. However, as the children discover themselves, they will find things of their own to occupy their time. Helping children to amuse themselves is one of the reasons for controlling TV, and parents should gradually cut back on the number of activities they plan for their children. Irritability can be reduced with outdoor play, an early bedtime, eating the right kind of food, and avoiding the wrong kind of food, especially too much sugar.

Parents should explain even to very young children why they cannot continue to watch as much TV. This is part of training them to base their own decisions on principle. One of the best settings for discussing the family's television habits, whether the children are younger or older, is during the evening devotional time. An evening Bible study hour has been a custom in my own home from the time the children were born. It has been a powerful influence in molding our children's moral attitudes, including their attitudes toward TV.

If several members of the family are addicted to TV, some may want to quit and others not. If you are the one who wants to quit, it is important that you use the right psychology. Avoid a holier-than-thou attitude. Do not pretend you are better than the rest, and never condemn them for their viewing habits. Avoid showing them magazine articles that condemn TV. It is better to leave the magazine in a prominent place and hope they will find it. Take the positive approach: look for other things to do yourself, such as going out with a friend or getting involved in some project outside the home. Give glowing reports of what you did, and after a few weeks invite your family to come along. Give them a taste of the fun of doing something outside the home, or something different in the home. For some people, that is all it takes.

If you and your family communicate well, try calling a family council and share your concern. After everyone is seated around the table or on the living room floor, start out something like this. "I've been thinking that we're missing out on some things in life because of TV. I wonder if anybody else has thought of the same thing." If you do not already know the answer to that question, you may be surprised. If you discover sympathy, ask their opinions. You will almost certainly find a reasonable compromise. If you do not find sympathy, you can hasten to explain that you are not suggesting getting rid of the TV, but simply finding a way to have a little more family life. You can suggest two things: (1) that the whole family choose certain programs to watch and then talk about when they are over; and (2) that the whole family decide on a certain time in the week when everybody will do something else together besides watching TV. Very few family members will object to a reasonable suggestion like that.

A family council may be planned, but often it works even better if it is spontaneous. And each day provides its own three opportunities: meal time. It can be over the breakfast table, or at lunch or dinner, whichever is the least hurried. One good way to bring up the subject is to say. "Let's do so-and so—" and suggest something for the whole family to do at a time when you are sure the TV will be on. Somebody is sure to object: "That's when I watch . . . ! We can't do it then." Your family council is in full swing. The suggestion was merely a technique to get things going, not an objective to argue over. Your next move can be, "I think we miss out on a lot of family togetherness because of TV. When would be a good time?" Be reasonable and you will almost certainly get a compromise.

One of the best ways to control TV is to watch with a

purpose, the way educators are learning to do. An objectionable program can be turned off, but it can also be analyzed. This method is particularly useful in the home where some family members differ with others over the value of certain programs. Instead of insisting that a teenager turn the set off, parents can cheerfully suggest that they watch it together and talk about it afterward. It is best for parents to avoid critical remarks about the moral implications of the program, especially the first few times they watch, since the teenager is likely to be sensitive about that. Discuss the plot and the merits of the way the characters in the story related to the dramatic situation. Above all, pray that God will open the way for the question of values to come up naturally. When it does, be casual. Get the teenager to express his views. You can differ with him cheerfully, objectively, and perhaps raise a non-threatening question to keep him thinking. Don't worry about what you will say when the time comes. God promises to give wisdom for that (James 1:5; Matthew 10:19).

Do not be too hasty about seeing progress. The least sign of a change in the teenager's attitude is a signal to keep trying. However, all is not lost if, after a reasonable time, the plan doesn't work. The teenager will see that you are willing to look at his point of view, and you can now suggest that he watch the objectionable program(s) in his own room . In some cases the teenager's sense of fairness toward the rest of the family will cause him to reject the idea. Also he may hold back from a proposition in which it seems that he is being excommunicated.

Television isn't bad. It isn't good, either. It's just a box with a screen and a few controls. The broadcast industry uses the medium to gain a profit. The result is programming that is in many instances far short of the Christian ideal. The Christian cannot turn the set on in the morning, leave it unattended all day, and expect the atmosphere of his home to be in harmony with the biblical ideal. Joshua told the Israelites, "Choose you this day whom ye will serve" (Joshua 24:15). Christians must choose the television programs that enter their homes. Their choices must be based on biblical principle, not impulse or whatever looks "good" in the *TV Guide*. And then they must control their sets to implement choices.

A TV out of control is like a temper out of control. It takes willpower to subdue. If you don't have enough, God has more, and He is happy to share. You must spend time with Him to get it. Study your Bible, pray, and ask God for help. Set your goals. Work toward them, continually asking God for help. You will be amazed what can happen in just one year's time.

You Can Help Change TV

The combined efforts of concerned parents, social scientists, and legislators brought the networks, in 1975, to curtail violence from the prime-time viewing hours. Change comes slowly, but if enough pressure is brought to bear it will come. If you would like to join other citizens in doing something to bring a more healthful atmosphere to network television, there are organizations that will welcome your help and that will suggest specific steps you can take. Write to:

Action for Children's Television
46 Austin Street
Newtonville, MA 02160

Committee on Children's Television
1511 Masonic Avenue
San Francisco, CA 94117

If you wish to write directly to the networks and the Federal Communications Commission, here are the addresses:

American Broadcasting Company (ABC)
1330 Avenue of the Americas
New York, NY 10019

Canadian Broadcasting Corporation (CBC)
1500 Bronson Avenue
Ottawa, Ontario, Canada K1G 3J5

Columbia Broadcasting System (CBS)
51 W. 52nd Street
New York, NY 10019

National Broadcasting Company (NBC)
30 Rockefeller Plaza
New York, NY 10020

Public Broadcasting Service (PBS)
15 W. 51st Street
New York, NY 10020

Federal Communications Commission (FCC)
1919 M Street, N.W.
Washington, D.C. 20554

Address all letters to the networks to *The President* or *The Director of Public Relations*. Your letter to the FCC should be addressed to *The Chairman*, Federal Communications Commission.

REFERENCES

Two sources quoted extensively in this book are abbreviated in these references. *TAT* refers to *Television Awareness Training*, Media Action Research Center, Inc., New York, 1976. *JC* refers to *Journal of Communication*, Autumn, 1975

CHAPTER 1

1. A widely quoted Neilsen figure, found even in highly professional literature, has young children (preschool) watching TV 54 hours a week. The Neilsen people say that's "an old misquote that keeps coming back to haunt" them. The actual figure is an average $23^{1}/_{4}$ hours a week for children two to five—considerably less than half the misquoted amount. See Claire Safran, "How TV Changes Children," *Redbook Magazine*, November 1975.

2. Figures are for 1975. See *TAT* 211; *Phi Delta Kappan*, November 1976, p. 180.

3. Ben Logan, "Has Anyone Seen the Teacher?" *TAT*, p. 229.

CHAPTER 2

1. Douglas Cater, *TV Violence and the Child: The Evolution and Fate of the Surgeon General's Report*. (New York: Russel Sage Foundation, 1975), p. 64.

2. "Fresh Crews Over Sixth Avenue," *Time*, October 31, 1977, p. 88.

3. Cater, *TV Violence and the Child*, p. 65.

4. David L. Bazelon, "As a Leading Jurist Sees the TV Industry," *TAT*, p. 295.

5. Quoted by Anne Somers, "Violence, Television, and the Health of American Youth," *New England Journal of Medicine*, April 8, 1976, p. 815.

6. "The Man With the Golden Gut," *Time*, September 5, 1977, p. 47.

7. Wendy Ehrlich, "The History of Children's Television," *Children's Television: The Economics of Exploitation* (New Haven: Yale University Press, 1973), p. 33.

CHAPTER 4

1. W. Andrew Collins, "The Developing Child as Viewer," *JC*, p. 41.
2. Robert M. Liebert and Rita Poulos, "Television as a Moral Teacher," *TAT*, p. 204.
3. *Ibid.*
4. Diane Liebert, "Television Advertising and Values," *TAT*, p. 69.
5. Elizabeth McCarthy, "Violence and Behavior Disorders," *JC*, pp. 81, 84.

CHAPTER 5

1. T. Morgan, *New York Times Magazine*, January 19, 1975, p. 11.
2. "The Youth Crime Plague," *Time*, July 11, 1977, p. 20.
3. *Ibid.*
4. John Camper, "Digest Computes Rate of Violence for Shows," *Fort Worth Star-Telegram*, March 17, 1976, p. 2-C.
5. Quoted by Anne R. Somers, "Violence, Television, and the Health of American Youth," *New England Journal of Medicine*, April 8, 1976, p. 814.
6. *Ibid.*
7. George Comstock, "The Evidence So Far," *JC*, p. 28.
8. Susan Harvey, "Television and Violence," *TAT*, p. 28.
9. Elizabeth D. McCarthy, "Violence and Behavior Disorders," *JC*, p. 74.
10. Ronald Drabman and Margaret Thomas, "Does TV Violence Breed Indifference?" *JC*, p. 74.
11. *Ibid.*, p. 87.
12. *Ibid.*, p. 88.
13. George Gerbner and Larry Gross, "Living with Television: The Violence Profile," *TAT*, pp. 223, 224.
14. *Ibid.*, p. 224.
15. Hayden Cameron, "Charles Bronson: Even I Am Shocked at Violence in Kids' TV Cartoons," *National Enquirer*, December 12, 1977, p. 39.

CHAPTER 6

1. Thomas F. Baldwin and Colby Lewis, *Television and Social Behavior*, vol. 1, p. 314, quoted in Douglas Cater, *TV Violence and the Child*, p. 60.
2. Cater, *TV Violence and the Child*, p. 61.
3. *Ibid.*, p. 97.
4. *Ibid.*

5. Michael B. Rothenberg, M.D., "Effect of Television Violence on Children and Youth," *Journal of the American Medical Association*, December 8, 1975, p. 1044.

6. Jesse Steinfeld, "TV Violence Is Harmful," *Reader's Digest*, May 1973, p. 38, quoted in Cater, *TV Violence and the Child*, p. 101.

7. Baldwin and Lewis, p. 354, quoted in Cater, p. 63.

8. Baldwin and Lewis, p. 307, quoted in Cater, p. 62.

9. Baldwin and Lewis, p. 349, quoted in Cater, p. 62.

10. As quoted by Michael B. Rothenberg. M.D., *op. cit.*, p. 1043.

11. Anne R. Somers, "Violence, Television, and the Health of American Youth," *New England Journal of Medicine*, April 8, 1976, pp. 814, 815.

12. *Ibid.*, p. 815.

13. "Fresh Crews Over Sixth Avenue," *Time*, October 31, 1977, p. 88.

CHAPTER 7

1. Thomas F. Baldwin and Colby Lewis, *Television and Social Behavior*, vol. 1, p. 314, quoted in Douglas Cater, *TV Violence and the Child*, p. 60.

2. Cater, pp. 61, 62.

CHAPTER 8

1. "More Sex, Less Violence: TV's New Pitch, *U.S. News and World Report*, September 12, 1977, p. 20.

2. "99 and $^{44}/_{100}$% Impure," *Newsweek*, June 13, 1977, p. 92.

3. *Ibid.*

4. *Ibid.*

5. "Tuesday Night on the Tube," *Time*, December 12, 1977, p. 94.

6. "TV Sex and Violence: Showdown Nears in Washington," *U.S. News and World Report*, January 13, 1975.

7. Susan Franzblau, "Television and Human Sexuality," *TAT*, pp. 112, 113.

CHAPTER 9

1. Robert Liebert and Rita Poulos, "Television as a Moral Teacher," *TAT*, p. 200.

2. Rita Poulos, Eli Rubinstein, Robert Liebert, "Positive Social Learning," *JC*, p. 90.

3. Ben Logan, "An Experiment in Positive TV Programming," *TAT*, p. 189.

4. *Ibid.*, p. 190.

5. Poulos, "Positive Social Learning," pp. 92-94.

6. Gerald Gorn, Marvin Goldberg, Rabindra Kanungo, "The Role of Educational Television in Changing the Intergroup Attitudes of Children," *Child Development*, March 1976, pp. 277-280.

CHAPTER 10

1. Facts and statistics taken from *Higher Education and National Affairs*, August 26, 1977, published by the American Council on Education, Washington, D.C.; and "Why Johnny Can't Read," *Newsweek*, December 8, 1975, pp. 58-65.

2. Werner Halpern, "Turned-on Toddlers," *JC*, pp. 66-70.

3. "Why Johnny Can't Write," *Newsweek*, December 8, 1975, p. 59.

4. *Ibid.*, p. 60.

5. *Ibid.*

6. "TV's Courtship of Turned-off Viewers," *U.S. News & World Report*, January 30, 1978, p. 54.

7. Joan Feeley, "Television and Reading in the Seventies," *Language Arts*, September 1975, pp. 797-801.

8. *Ibid.*, p. 798.

9. Max Gunther, "How Television Helps Johnny Read," *TV Guide*, September 4, 1976, pp. 6, 7.

10. Anne Adams and Cathy Harrison, "Using Television to Teach Specific Reading Skills," *The Reading Teacher*, October 1975, p. 45.

CHAPTER 11

1. Thomas Kuncl, "Breaking a Child of the TV Habit Is Like Trying to Cure a Drug Addict," *National Enquirer*, November 22, 1977, p. 8.